MW00619999

WHITE LILIES

WHITE LILIES
Letters, Conversations,
& Poems from Prison

Valeriu Gafencu

Translation, Introduction,
& Notes by Octavian Gabor

Saint Tikhon's
Monastery Press

MMXXII

White Lilies: *Letters, Conversations, & Poems from Prison*
Valeriu Gafencu, author
Octavian Gabor, translator and editor

ISBN: 978-1-7361723-6-0

First Impression, April, 2022.

Cover Illustration by Hierodeacon Marc (Romanchak)

CONTENTS

Introduction

"NEVER THINK THAT YOU ARE WORTHLESS"

VALERIU Gafencu was born on January 24, 1921, in Sângerei, a village in Bessarabia.[1] He died in a communist political prison at the age of thirty-one, on February 18, 1952.[2] He was arrested in 1941 for

1 Bessarabia had become part of Romania three years prior to Gafencu's birth. In March 27, 1918, the legislative body of the Moldavian Democratic Republic voted for union with Romania. This land, between the rivers of Prut and Dnieper, was incorporated to Russia in 1812, after the Napoleonic Wars. The Moldavian Republic was constituted in 1917, after it proclaimed its independence from Russia, following the Bolshevik Revolution. Bessarabia was occupied by Soviet forces once again in June 1940.

2 The communists took power in Romania after the Second World War, with the support of the Red Army and after falsified elections. They imprisoned the leaders of the traditional parties and, according to Fr. George Calciu (see *Interviews, Homilies, and Talks*. Saint Herman of Alaska Brotherhood, 2010), an entire generation of intellectuals. Being openly atheistic, the communists also persecuted people of faith. Fr.

belonging to the Brotherhood of the Cross,[3] a youth
organization of the Legionary movement, which was
associated with the Antisemitism that plagued Eu-
rope during the first half of the 20th century. According to Ioan Ianolide, one of Gafencu's close friends
and also a legionary, the Brotherhood of the Cross
didn't have a political purpose but was involved with
the Christian and national education of the youth.[4]
The Legionary movement had been outlawed by
Marshal Ion Antonescu, the head of the Romanian
government, after the Legionary Rebellion in January
1941.[5] Gafencu spent more than a third of his life—

George Calciu spent 21 years in prison. He was first arrested
in 1948, when he was still a medical student, for his standing
"against the introduction of Marxism and Bolshevism as the
only philosophy taught in schools" (Father George Calciu,
op. cit., p. 32). He was released in 1964, when the communist
government issued a general amnesty. In 1979 he was arrested
a second time, after a series of seven homilies delivered during
Great Lent, which were considered hostile by the communist
regime. He was released in 1984, after political pressure from
the government of the USA.

3   "Frăția de cruce," in Romanian. It could also be translated as
     Blood Brotherhood, as Roland Clark does in his *Holy Legion-
     ary Movement: Fascist Activism in Interwar Romania* (Ithaca,
     NY: Cornell University Press, 2015).

4   See Ioan Ianolide, *Întoarcerea la Hristos: document pentru
     o lume nouă* [The Return to Christ: Document for a New
     World] (București: Bonifaciu, 2012), 42. Ianolide's volume is
     the source for Gafencu's poems and letters contained in this
     volume.

5   For more on the history of the Legionary movement in Ro-
     mania, see Roland Clark, op.cit.

hence his entire adult life—in political prisons. He never held public office. When he was imprisoned at the age of twenty, he was a student at the University of Iași, where, as he remembered in one of his letters from prison, "I lived a normal life, and I was one of the most appreciated students, loved by everyone, and I had an unusual thirst for the Ideal: a new world, in which love and justice, perfect harmony, would reign."[6] Nevertheless, his name continues to engender controversies among the people of Romania to this day. On the one hand, the testimonies of those who encountered him in prison depict him as a saint. Ioan Ianolide focuses his book, *Intoarcerea la Hristos,* on Gafencu's personality. Octavian Anastasescu, who met Gafencu at the political prison in Târgu Ocna, towards the end of Gafencu's life, says, "My duty to Valeriu Gafencu is so great that I must tell someone who he was for me and that I do not regret the extreme suffering I experienced during one year and eleven months."[7] Nicolae Steinhardt, who was baptized in secret in a political prison, called him one of the saints of the prisons, although he never personally met Gafencu.[8] On the other hand,

6   See below, p. 40.
7   Octav Anastasescu, *Lângă Valeriu Gafencu, sfântul închisorilor: Mărturia unui fost socialist* [With Valeriu Gafencu, the Saint of Prisons: The Testimony of a Former Socialist] (București: Areopag, 2014), 23.
8   See Nicolae Steinhardt, *Jurnalul fericirii* [The Diary of Happiness] (Rohia: Editura Manastirii Rohia, 2005).

his involvement in the Brotherhood of the Cross and, by consequence, his association with the Legionary movement[9] places a shade over his life that encourages others to throw his memory into the dungeons of history.

While the crimes of Legionaries have well been documented by historians,[10] Gafencu was not directly responsible for them. The discussion of the responsibility that is shared by a movement and the individuals who, at various moments during their lives, embrace an idea is a difficult and interesting one, but it is not within the scope of this volume. The twentieth century was marred by two criminal ideologies: fascism and communism, and the evil nature of these ideologies and the responsibilities of all individuals must be acknowledged; historians of both movements have done important work and continue to do so.

At the same time, rejecting anything that comes

9   For an analysis of the Legionary movement, see Roland Clark's *Holy Legionary Youth: Fascist Activism in Interwar Romania*. Gafencu was never a part of the political party that stemmed from the Legionary movement, but he was arrested in connection with his activities as part of the Brotherhood of the Cross, an organization that provided the basis of the movement and sought spiritual revival. Octav Anastasescu states in his memoirs, *Lângă Valeriu Gafencu, sfântul închisorilor*, that Gafencu "never wore the Legionary coat. He began and he finished with the Brotherhood of the Cross" (62).

10 See, for example, Clark's *Holy Legionary Movement: Fascist Activism in Interwar Romania*.

from a person due to only one aspect of his life seems problematic and certainly against an Orthodox Christian *ethos*. We are not judging a human life based on what was a mistake, especially when one paid for it with years of prison—in fact, with one's entire adult life. Gafencu was imprisoned when he was twenty years old. He spent in prison his remaining eleven years of life, and this volume brings forward his writing during that time. Whatever his thoughts and actions may have been prior to that, he paid for them with his suffering.

If anything, Valeriu Gafencu's story reminds that the roots of good and evil are in our human heart, and we participate in them voluntarily or blindly. As Mitya says emphatically in Dostoevsky's *The Brothers Karamazov*, a human's heart "can be aglow with the perfection of the Madonna [...] and still he won't renounce Sodom."[11] Nevertheless. Gafencu's life produced lilies as beautiful as the poems that you will find in this volume. Without denying his participation in the darkness of this world—"in sins my mother conceived me"[12]—the volume remains a testimony of the beauty one can produce in darkness. Gafencu's words are a testimony to his suffering and to the joy experienced in it; they do not provide a justification of what came prior to them. They may, nevertheless,

11 F. M. Dostoevsky, *The Brothers Karamazov*, (Oxford: Oxford University Press, 1994), 136.

12 Psalm 51:5 (LXX 50:5).

offer inspiration, just as they offered moral support to Gafencu's colleagues in prison, who memorized his poems and transmitted them by word of mouth.

Gafencu lived in a time of turmoil. The Second World War started when he was eighteen years old. The political climate in Romania was in a state of agitation. After the secret Molotov-Ribbentrop Pact between Nazi Germany and the Soviet Union,[13] the region of Bessarabia was annexed by the Soviet Union in June, 1940, while a large part of Transylvania was annexed by Hungary, an ally of Germany at the time. Gafencu's family—his mother and three sisters—fled Bessarabia to what was left of Romania, taking refuge in the city of Iași. His father remained in Bessarabia, refusing to leave the land he loved, and was deported by the Soviets to Siberia, where he died one year later. Valeriu took law courses at the University of Iași, "appreciated by professors and loved by colleagues and friends, being a model of humble and pure behavior."[14]

Ioan Ianolide recalls, "We were floating in some confusion, since we were formed in times of persecution, having no guides, having no literature. We had only one sublime ideal, toward which we sin-

---

13   See Roger Moorhouse, *The Devils' Alliance: Hitler's Pact with Stalin*, 1939–1941 (New York: Basic Books, 2014).

14   Moise Iorgovan, *Sfântul închisorilor* (Alba Iulia, 2007), 17–18. The volume was published in English: *Monk Moise, The Saint of the Prisons: Notes on the life of Valeriu Gafencu, collected and annotated by the monk Moise* (Triada, 2019).

cerely aspired, being spiritually inspired."[15] Ianolide also emphasizes the youthfulness of Gafencu and his friends when they were imprisoned:

> We were young people, who were born between 1920 and 1930, and so we never had a political or public function, and therefore bore no responsibility for the events of this century. We had the conviction that we were not involved in politics, but in education. We desired to form an elite of high purpose, which could take into its own hands the destiny of the Romanian people.[16]

If we are to read the testimonies of those who encountered Gafencu and knew him, we find stories that seem to come down from the lives of saints. In prison Valeriu "continued to engage in the education of youth, but he also contemplated grave and serious problems of conscience."[17] The crucial moment of Gafencu's spiritual life, as Ianolide calls it, came one day in June 1943,[18] when he fell, face on the ground, and cried out, "I am the most sinful man!"[19] Remembering this moment in one of his letters, Gafencu says, "I had buried every precious thing that God had sown in me into the earth of my sins. I feel respon-

15   Ioan Ianolide, *Intoarcerea la Hristos*, 33.
16   Ibid., 33.
17   Ibid., 43.
18   This is the date mentioned in one of the letters he sent home—see below, p. 33.
19   Ioan Ianolide, *Intoarcerea la Hristos*, 43.

sible for all the sins of my brothers, from all times
and all places, because I have disregarded this holy
gift, love."[20] It is this gift, love, which was witnessed
by everyone who met Gafencu in prison.

Father George Calciu, twice imprisoned by the
communists for a sum of more than twenty years,
met Gafencu two or three times.[21] He says,

> It was enough just to see him and to pass by him, to
> immediately feel the influence of Gafencu. ... He
> might have spent time with four hundred differ-
> ent people as they moved through his cell.[22] The
> moment they were in the cell with Gafencu, they
> completely forgot any bad thought, any rebellion

20   See below, p. 34.
21   George Calciu, *Interviews, Homilies, and Talks* (Platina, Ca-
     lif.: St. Herman of Alaska Brotherhood, 2010), 136.
22   Calciu probably refers to Room Four in Târgu Ocna, where
     those who had tuberculosis were brought to spend their final
     days. In his book, *In God's Underground* (Bartlesville, OK:
     Living Sacrifice Book Company, 2004), Richard Wurmbrand
     refers to the same room. Those familiar with the stories
     of communist persecution may notice that there were two
     famous instances of a Room Four in the constellation of
     political prisons. One was in Piteşti prison, where the terrible
     experiment known as the Piteşti Phenomenon was conducted,
     in which students were forced to torture other students, their
     own friends, so that their souls would be forever transformed.
     It was a process of separation, in which each human being
     disappeared as person, in losing all connections with his
     brethren. Room Four in Târgu Ocna was its opposite:
     spiritually and physically broken people came to die here, but
     they recovered their spiritual being under the influence of
     Valeriu Gafencu.

against Jesus Christ. A church was established in the cell. There were young people, rebellions, conflicts, and so on, but he changed their soul and their mind. Therefore his memory is greatly revered, and the people who stayed with him in the same room still pray to him as to a saint."[23]

During one of the nights spent at the prison hospital in Târgu-Ocna, where the people who had tuberculosis were brought to live their last days, Valeriu Gafencu confessed to his friend, Ioan Ianolide, an encounter with the Mother of the Lord, which I will cite here:

> I was awake, lucid, and serene, when I realized I was holding Seta's picture in my hand [Seta was the girl with whom he was in love].[24] Surprised by this, I raised my eyes, and I saw the Mother of the Lord, dressed in white, standing, alive, real. She was without the Child. Her presence seemed material. The Mother of the Lord was truly next to me. And I was filled with joy. I had forgotten everything. Time seemed unending. She then told me: "I am your love! Do not be afraid. Do not doubt. The victory will be my Son's. He sanctified this place for the things that will come. The powers of darkness will increase and will continue

---

23   George Calciu, *Interviews, Homilies, and Talks*, 136.
24   Valeriu Gafencu was taken into prison when he was only 20 years old. Years later, he learned that Seta had since married.

to frighten the world, but they will be shattered.
My Son is waiting for people to turn to faith. Today, the sons of darkness have more courage than
the sons of light. ... But take heart, the world is
Christ's."[25]

The embrace of the Mother of God is one of the
recurrent themes of political prison testimonies. She
is the protector of those who have lost all hope. It is
to her that they turn in prayer because she receives
all. Rejected by the world and accused for their beliefs, the inmates of communist prisons often found
that the one they could turn to was Mary, the Mother who never leaves her sons. Having no informa-
tion from home—the authorities severed all possible connections the prisoners had with the outside
world—and being told that their own families had
turned their backs on them, the youths turned to the
Mother of the Lord and prayed to her for comfort.
There was a connection between, on the one hand,
those who were made empty through external violence and, on the other hand, Mary, the one who
emptied herself out of Love. This connection could
afford them the possibility of turning the dirt that
their lives had become into fertile ground.[26]

25   Ioan Ianolide, *Întoarcerea la Hristos*, 180. The passage is remi-
      niscent of John 16:30.

26   See Anthony Bloom's discussion on the humility of the earth
      in his *Beginning to Pray* (New York, Mayway, NJ: Paulist
      Press, 1970), 35.

Valeriu Gafencu had become just such fertile ground through the humility of his heart. Richard Wurmbrand remembers Gafencu in his writings about the persecutions that he himself suffered. Wurmbrand explains Gafencu's saintly attitude in prison by claiming that, "like other Iron Guard followers[27] in whom Christian belief had prevailed, he could not do enough to make up for his mistakes."[28] Wurmbrand continues,

> Every day, he set the example of putting aside part of his meager ration to help build up the weakest among us. His Antisemitism had been left behind, and when some of his old fascist friends came to see him in Room Four, he suddenly came out with a remark that shocked them: "I'd like to see the country ruled entirely by Jews... They must be men like the old Jewish rulers, like Joseph, Moses, Daniel, Peter, Paul, and Jesus himself. Because if

27 Wurmbrand mistakenly claims that Gafencu was a former Iron Guard trooper; see *In God's Underground*, 84. Gafencu never joined the Iron Guard, the political wing of the Legionary movement.

28 Wurmbrand, *In God's Underground*, 89. Wurmbrand seems to assume that Gafencu's mistakes were political. I think Gafencu was speaking rather about mistakes that stem from an attitude not rooted in love.

we have any more Jews over us like Ana Pauker,[29] then Romania is finished."[30]

Wurmbrand was himself a Jew who had become a protestant Christian before being imprisoned. During the war, he suffered persecution as a Jew. When the war ended, the new authorities persecuted him as a Christian. His words about Gafencu, with whom he had long dialogues, according to testimonies,[31] show a man transfigured by faith. In appearance, Gafencu was the shadow of a human being. He could no longer lie back because it was too painful. "Every day he had a little less control over his body, often fulfilling his necessities where he lay; then having to wait, sometimes at night for hours, until someone came to clean him."[32] Still, despite all this, Gafencu never complained.

29   Ana Pauker was a leader of the Communist Party in Romania immediately after WWII and the country's foreign minister during the first years of the totalitarian regime.

30   Ibid., 89.

31   See Ianolide, *Întoarcerea la Hristos*, 158–78, and Anastasescu, *Lângă Valeriu Gafencu*, 63–66. According to both these testimonies, Gafencu saved Wurmbrand's life. Gafencu contracted tuberculosis (TBC) while he was imprisoned. Someone smuggled in some streptomycin, which was the hope of the prisoners with TBC. Ianolide and Anastasescu claim that Gafencu did not take the streptomycin, instead he offered it to Wurmbrand. This episode is not mentioned in Wurmbrand's book.

32   Wurmbrand, *In God's Underground*, 90.

Gafencu died on February 18, 1952. Ianolide remembers the event in the following words:

> That day, I experienced the feeling that the mysteries of creation were revealed, that the soles of my feet had beneath them some sort of cloth that sustained me, and the soul had the feeling of plenitude. I was so joyful during those hours that I will never forget it. I do not desire a state higher than the one from that day, even in eternity, because I was full, completely happy. I believe that Christ was present in Valeriu. This is the only way in which I can explain his state of grace, as well as my and our friends' amazement.[33]

When Gafencu died, his fellow prisoners knelt and prayed.[34] Wurmbrand remembers his own thoughts:

> Jesus tells us that if a seed does not fall into the earth and die, it cannot bring forth fruit, and that as a seed is reborn in a beautiful flower, so man dies and his mortal body is renewed in a spiritual body. And his heart which has come to be filled with the Spirit of Christ will surely bear fruit.[35]

33   Ianolide, *Întoarcerea la Hristos,* 189.
34   Wurmbrand, *In God's Underground,* 90.
35   Ibid., 90.

I have often heard people wondering what they would have done if they had lived during the communist era: would they have become persecutors or informants for the secret police? Would they have had the strength to resist the temptation to save themselves at the expense of their fellow human beings? The same question appears when people discuss the Holocaust or other horrific events in the history of humanity. What would I have done had I lived during those times?

The question can easily become a way to tell ourselves that we are better than others. Few of us are able to say that we may have been an agent of the secret police, a prison guard, a torturer, or a Nazi officer. Our firm belief in our moral strength does not allow us to consider this possibility. At other times, however, the question becomes agonizing, because it reveals to us that the world is not so clearly divided between good and evil, and because we discover that we might not have had the power to sacrifice convenience for truth. We acknowledge, in these moments, that we are rather weak before that "voice of reason" which tells us that we owe it to ourselves to remain alive, regardless of the means to do so. This "voice of reason" comes slowly and progressively; we are rarely in the situation in which we need to choose between pure good and evil. Instead, we perceive ourselves as human beings in connection with others and so we believe that it is safe to do what others do, to show, at least, that we think like them because we wish to be accepted and thus somehow protected. Actions that we consider glorious in stories may appear to us in a different light in such moments: they become irrational. A few examples may suffice. Is it rational to say that you still believe in God if this statement produces hatred in your torturer to the point where you are left in a pool of blood? Is it rational to say no to collaboration with the secret police when you are threatened with your family's suffering and when you notice that many of your friends are already collaborators? Is it rational to leave behind everything you have and go into the mountains to form a resistance movement and thus live as an outcast with a death sentence on your head? Is it rational to give your piece of bread to your fellow inmate when you are yourself on the brink of death by starvation?

Many of us may say that all such acts are instead an expression of our folly, and we would recognize that the power of "reason" convinces us to be what we despise when we read stories of persecution: the torturers themselves, or perhaps people who witnessed horrors and said nothing.

Regardless of the way in which we answer the question, "What would I have done?" it is a rather fruitless enterprise, because it leads to separation from our own self. We disappear from the present and move into a realm that we cannot change, much less understand. We lose the possibility of being present to the world that is given to us in this moment. And so, when discussing communist persecution and the different ways in which Romanians responded to it between 1946 and 1989, one cannot proceed without careful introspection. To think about terror is to think about how one would respond to life in each and every moment: by focusing on self-preservation or by giving one's life to the other. And so, wherever one lives, one's life can bear fruit.

In one of Valeriu Gafencu's letters written from prison, he ends with these words, "Beloved brother, never think that you are worthless. Wherever you are, it's by God's will; and you have a call to answer."[36] Fr. Iustin Pârvu, who was also imprisoned by the communist regime in Romania, said, "None of the hours of suffering in prison was useless."[37]

If you are not to consider yourself useless, then you cannot consider yourself a victim, either. However—this is the case especially when we discuss persecution—we tend to say that those destroyed by violence and terror are victims. And we often pity them. We often pity ourselves as well because we are thrown into a life that we believe we do not deserve, or because we experience events that we believe diminish our possibility of realizing the full potential of our lives.

36   See below, p. 46.
37   Words spoken by Fr. Pârvu in interview given after the fall of communism.

We often say that people are victims when they encounter events that they do not deserve. Armed with a conception of justice that we uphold, we can even say that Jesus was unjustly murdered, and that his murderers deserve punishment. Or that communism destroyed lives, and those who implemented a communist regime thus deserve to be punished. We have become the knowers of God's justice and we want to implement it everywhere around us. We thus transform ourselves into observers of a world that we can judge. We no longer find it acceptable to just live as part of this world for which we are responsible, and of which we are not the judge, forgetting thus that a shepherd does not judge his flock.[38]

In his life, as it is expressed in his poems and letters, Gafencu reminded us that we have a call to answer. It may sound heroic, as if the salvation of the world rested upon our shoulders. If this is how we understand it, then we are in the danger of becoming vigilantes. But Gafencu was not speaking from such a perspective. There is nothing heroic about this call, at least not if we consider the usual use of the word "heroic." Having a call to answer may mean washing dishes when they are dirty; it may mean listening to a family member when he or she talks to us; it may

38   In his 51st homily, St. Isaac the Syrian says, "Mercy and justice in one soul is like a man who worships God and the idols in one house." *The Ascetical Homilies of St. Isaac the Syrian* (Boston, Mass.: Holy Transfiguration Monastery, 2011) 379.

mean always being present in the moment that is giv-
en to us, regardless of that moment, and not dream
of a parallel, distant, or future life. The call requires
our presence. It wants us to live. Gafencu reveals how
this could be understood: the purpose of man is "to
love all of God's creation and to do good."[39]

This edition brings together some of the letters, dialogues, and poems written by Valeriu Gafencu, as
they appeared in Ioan Ianolide's volume, *Întoarcerea
la Hristos: document pentru o lume nouă*.[40] The letters and poems were written while Gafencu was in
prison, where he went through the spiritual transformation that is documented in one of his letters.
Ioan Ianolide's volume was published by Bonifaciu
Publishing House of the Diaconești Monastery in
Romania. The guide for confession attributed to
Valeriu Gafencu, which was published in Moise Iorgovan's *Sfântul Închisorilor* (*The Saint of Prisons*), is
also included here.

   According to Ianolide, Gafencu wrote 16 poems
in prison, during the last part of his life. Ianolide says,
"He had no paper or pencil, but he composed them
in his mind and memorized them. Then, they were
learned by friends and transmitted forward."[41] The

39   Ioan Ianolide, *Întoarcerea la Hristos*, 225.
40   Romanian: The Return to Christ: A Document for a New
     World.
41   Ianolide, *Întoarcerea la Hristos*, 241.

poems of this volume are those that Ianolide himself included in his *Intoarcerea la Hristos.*[42] Ianolide also mentions Valeriu's own words about his poetry: "Here, in Târgu-Ocna, I wrote sixteen poems as a testament, as a real confession for those who will come after me. I pray you to not interpret this poetry as a figure of style, because it is ardent and living spirit."

The eight poems that follow are published in both Romanian and English. The letters from prison appear only in translation.

I am much indebted to Mark Klus for reading this volume prior to publication and offering helpful and timely advice. Fr. John Mikitish supported and advised me in various stages of this work. Fr. John was the one with whom the structure of this volume was conceived. This work benefited from the suggestions offered by Ioana Haşu-Georgiev, Georgi Georgiev, Constanţa Moşoiu, and Adrian Olteanu. I am grateful for their contributions and for their unconditional friendship.

I could have never engaged in this work without the support of my wife, Elena, and my son, Andrei. They have often suggested the right term whenever I could not find it. They are the ones who, day by day, bring to life white lilies in my existence.

—Octavian Gabor

42   I have tried to find other poems, but to no success. There are some poems that circulate over the Internet and are attributed to Valeriu Gafencu, but I chose to only translate those mentioned by Ianolide in his volume.

REMEMBERING VALERIU GAFENCU

by Ioan Ianolide

VALERIU died thirty-one years ago today. I went to church and had confession. I will go to communion on Sunday.

That day of holiness is built into my being, and nothing can separate me from it. It remains the happiest day of my life, although the human being dearest to me was passing from this life. But it was he who, on that day, transferred to me the state of inner fullness that continues to be with me even today. I think I was in heaven. I think I was next to Christ, because Christ was present in Valeriu. Valeriu's faith gave me strength. Valeriu's love subjected me fully to Christ's love.

Even if I am sick in body, even if my nerves are over-sensitive, my mind is unharmed and clear. I have isolated myself because the people of the world reject me or attack me, and this is the only way in which I can defend myself from them. I live alone, in silence.

I perceive the spiritual, political, social, economical, and military disaster the world is in, and I don't believe that it can be fixed. The world suffers the consequences of its erroneous direction, and this will not change before its mind opens toward the acceptance of the truth of God and of faith. This is why faith must have authentic confessors.

I know that the world is circumscribed by the divine economy of salvation. I believe. I love. I hope.

Today, just as thirty-one years ago, I feel I am next to Valeriu and, together with him, next to Christ the Lord.

Letters

Please send me my courses in Law. I want to study. Also, a German language course, because I want to study German well. ...[1] I am spiritually content, and I am at peace with myself. I'm not lying to you. It is the reality of my soul, which found its peace in the understanding and the help of Almighty God. I believe that man can find peace in his soul only through the truth of the Gospels.

My darling, dear sisters, I pray you, be vigilant against sin, live in purity, because this is the only way in which you will be victorious in life!

---

[1]   The ellipses are in the Romanian edition, which does not explain whether it was Ianolide's choice or that of the editors. Ianolide says in his short introduction that these are fragments of his letters.

August 1942

I came down with jaundice. Your letters have enliv-
ened me. I miss home and freedom. ... Spiritually
I am well. God guides me and, to me, his light is a
torch eternally lit. Pray incessantly.

September 1, 1942

My thoughts fly toward beautiful Bessarabia. ... As
for you, bring your hearts as close as possible to God,
for only in Him does one find salvation.

October 14, 1942

I feel alone here in the life of this accursed world. I
spend time having God in my mind, always. Only
God understands me fully, and, to my great spiritual
contentment, I sense him close to me eternally, pro-
tecting me and illuminating my path. I am so filled
with joy whenever I feel the Christian spirit vibrat-
ing within. You may never understand this!

There are so few people who understand Christ;
those who live him are even fewer. Faith is everything in life. This is why a man without faith is dead.

November 1, 1942

The fact that I have reached the point of understanding, even living, the teaching of Christ has made me

to feel content and as if awoken from the tomb. It has been the solitude, the life that I have, and the natural abstinence that follows this, that have contributed to this. I sometimes think that I would have never arrived at such an inner transformation in a normal life.

June 21, 1943

A great day! I went to confession, and I had communion. I am experiencing great moments, the greatest of my life! It is a crossroad in my life! I have given myself fully to the will of God.

January 10, 1944

There are so many souls, Lord, that desire to live a new life, in which peace, understanding, and Christian love would reign! ... Every day is equal to a lifetime of happiness! I pray to the good God to give me the power to do the good that my soul desires to do in the world. I believe that this is the meaning of man's life: to love God's entire creation and to do good.

February 10, 1945

As long as God watches over the world, no evil can shake the moral and deeply Christian ground of pure souls, which are filled with the unbounded love for truth and one's neighbor.

Suffering, regardless of how difficult it is, has no other meaning than the purification of the soul that desires salvation. ... I desire to know that you[2] are ready to receive the most difficult blows while you have faith that, beyond this passing life, there is another life, eternal, joyful, a heavenly country without borders, which deserves any sacrifice, no matter how great it would be.

I am healthy and happy. Nothing could ruin this spiritual state. I am so happy that I would shout from all my being, so that all people would hear my cry, even Tuța[3] from where he is, so that my happiness would reach heaven!

2   Gafencu addresses his sisters.

3   Tuța refers to Valeriu Gafencu's father. The word comes from tătuța, which is already a diminutive of tata, father. The short form increases the sense of endearment. Virgil Maxim recounts the scene when Valeriu saw his father for the last time. It was in 1940, when Bessarabia was handed over to the Soviet Union, as a consequence of the secret pact between Ribbentrop and Molotov. Valeriu's father helped his family cross the river Prut, which was now separating Romania from Bessarabia. Then, after a short rest, he told his son that he would have to take care of his mother and his three sisters from that moment on. He was ready to go back to Bessarabia. Gafencu's family crossed the river Prut to Romania after Bessarabia was annexed by the Soviet Union. Valeriu's father, however, returned to Bessarabia, because he could not refuse taking part in the suffering that was awaiting his people. Here are his words, as they appear in Monk Moise Iorgovan's volume, *Sfântul Închisorilor*: "What would all of our Bessarabian

February 20, 1945

The Mother of the Lord fulfills my prayers. I live on the overflowing of true waves of love, which overwhelm my entire being that is penetrated by the conscientiousness of my own human nothingness on earth. I remain fallen on my knees before an icon, imploring for mercy, help, and love for me and for all of my people: parents, relatives, friends, benefactors, enemies.[4] ... I am as you know me. I don't say a word, but rather meditate for hours and days. I send my thoughts far away, and when I wake to reality, I smile. I sing and I pray. I am joyful spiritually. Daily life has a uniform aspect. My inner life is simple, intense, large, and filled with longings and dreams that I experience and that are alive within my soul.

---

brothers say? How could I raise my eyes to heaven if I and others like me, who until now have struggled to preserve the Romanian spirit in this land, would now flee from the path of the oppressors and not take part in the suffering that awaits us?" (The volume has appeared in Romanian; the translation I am using here is done by Monk Sava from Oasa Monastery—not yet published, to my knowledge).

4   Here is the prisoners' prayer for their enemies in the Aiud prison: "Lord, Jesus Christ, who suffered for the entire human race and who has forgiven all who repented their sins, protect us from causing any harm to those who hate and persecute us at your judgment. Rather, turn their souls toward the conscience [sic] of truth and give them true repentance, so that your holy Name may be glorified through them as well. And make us worthy, Lord, to confess you, the true God, Father, Son, and Holy Spirit, to the glory of your Name and the salvation of our souls! Amen."

I am fighting against my sins. As I go deeper with-in me, I discover new ones, again and again. But, with the Lord's help, I conquer them. I have acquired a lasting spiritual serenity, and I am content with the gifts God has given me, for they are priceless. I con-fess the same thing again: I experience happiness, I taste it especially in tears and pain, because it is there that I find it to be sweeter and deeper. I have the con-science of a sinful man. I experience God, the spring of all life's joys. ... I am very content now that I have lived a moral and pure life. In my relationships with girls, I was honest, correct, and pure; more precise-ly, I did not fall into sin. And I have loved so much! ... I'm telling you directly: I am happy. I understand and forgive everything; I forgive anyone who would harm me personally.

April 10, 1945

Simplify your lives as much as possible! Get used to being content with little, to sacrifice yourself for your neighbor's well-being! ... Prayer is the purest ex-pression of one's love for God and for one's neighbor. When you achieve true prayer, you have attained peace, happiness.

May 25, 1945

I am telling you as seriously as possible: examine your conscience as carefully as possible; examine your life well, and go deep within your being so that you know yourselves, with all your sins and errors committed during your life. Write them down and go before your spiritual father and confess them. It is never too late, but do not postpone this even for a day!

I speak to you as your son and brother,[5] with all the love that I have for you. I speak with the conviction of my soul, not from books, but from my own experience during these recent years, the most serious and important years of my life, which for me represent everything, absolutely everything. ... I thank the Good Lord with all my heart for the suffering He has sent to me. Through suffering, I could illumine my soul and find the path of life.

I implore you from my heart to read the Holy Scriptures. Every evening before bed, gather together around mom, you, dear children of my heart, and serenely reconnect with yourselves for a few moments and read a chapter from the Gospel, a chapter from the Epistles, and a psalm. Then, with much devotion, recite your evening prayers. ... It would be very well if you had a candle in your bedroom. In silence, with a lit candle, each one of you should examine her deeds, thoughts, and words that you may have said and done during the day. When you realize an error, confess it immediately with honesty, asking for forgiveness. Then... sleep well! ...

Love one another with all your being! Always

5   Valeriu Gafencu was writing to his mother and sisters.

help one another! My beloved, this would be the greatest and finest thing you could accomplish: a Christian family. May a troubled heart find comfort among you!

June 25, 1945

You should know that I am not worried about your fate for one reason: I know you are pure at heart, with faith in God, and with love for all. These great realities give me full confidence that you will conquer all the trials that you will encounter in the future. Analyze things in depth. Don't you see that God has sent you various trials to strengthen your faith? Don't you taste a joy that springs from the inner world of your spiritual being during the most difficult moments? A new happiness, found in tears. ... I desire so much to be among you, to come through in the intimacy of your souls, and to open widely the doors of the love which dreams and waits within you for the moment when it can overflow in waves; to see you bursting into tears of joy, kneeling before the icon of Christ, confessing your sins and being thankful. ...

Listen to the voice of your conscience always, living in truth with the fullness of your souls. I want to know that you are serene and fully aware of the purpose that you have as living beings: salvation. I want to know that you are pure in heart. A virginal purity, filled with virtue. Be Christian in your way of life!

September 23, 1945

Prayer is the purest expression of one's love for God and neighbor. When you are able to pray truly, you will know peace and happiness. I try again and again, and the good God protects me and gives me so much that I see a miracle at every step. I must be honest and confess that I accomplish very little, that I do not yet pray with my heart cleansed of worries, sins, and worldly thoughts. Dear Norica,[6] only the one who has tasted the deep joys of one's soul can understand them. I have had moments during life when I cried with inextinguishable tears, realizing the futility and the nothingness of my human nature, the glory of God, and his love. Well, in these tears springing from the depth of my grieved being, I found the highest and purest happiness that I have ever experienced. I would be so happy to achieve a continual state of prayer! ... This life is completely fleeting. And everything that belongs to it is fleeting as well!

November 20, 1945

I am especially concerned with the problem of sin. Since June 1943, when I experienced the first spiritual shaking that stemmed from becoming aware of

6   Norica is one of Gafencu's sisters.

sin, I realized that I discover new sins as I go deeper within me.

In the inmost depths of my heart I have found the inexhaustible spring of life, love. I realized that I have neglected this gift. I then said, "I was wrong!" I had buried in the earth of my sins everything precious that God had sown in me. I feel responsible for all the sins of my brothers, from all times and all places, because I have disregarded this holy gift, love. But I am a blessed man, the most blessed man! I feel God's love, his protection, and his care for me at every step. I want to no longer live for myself, but for love; I want to contribute to everyone's happiness, with the gift of God. I want to save my soul in the salvation of my brethren. How happy I am! How can man, this small being, experience so much happiness?

Man's life is a priceless gift, a miracle, and I strive to become like a little child.[7] After thousands of sufferings, I accomplished the most beautiful friendship of my life. We will live our entire life one for the other, heavenly King!

Christmas, 1945

It is night. I just read the Akathist to the Lord. My Christmas was more beautiful than a fairytale!

Spiritually, I felt I was more prepared than at other times. Because of the weight of the sufferings that

7　Mt. 18:3.

I have experienced for the resurrection of the soul, I felt strongly the responsibility I have for the salvation of my soul, my family, relatives, friends, enemies, and the entire nation.

As I was moving up on the letter of the ideal, I perceived myself smaller, more sinful, and the ideal higher and more perfect: Christ!

And, step by step, all the idols of my adolescence were demolished. The veil was lifted from my eyes by the fight with sin, and the living, serene icon of the Lord Jesus Christ was the only thing that remained before me!

Thus have we succeeded in establishing peace with all of our brethren, only by trampling ourselves underfoot, by acknowledging our sins, and by loving. I felt so much peace on Friday, facing the priest! Many of us received communion. What a great day, what a beautiful day! I experienced it to the fullest, with all the blessings that God has sent me![8]

New Year, 1946

White flowers sing at the gate of the heart. Whoever has lived divine love will understand me and will be happy for my happiness. ... I have prepared myself and I continue to prepare to become a Christian. Man is not saved in the monastery only. ... The

---

8   A carol follows here. It has been re-located to the poetry sections, under the title: A Star from the East.

helplessness of human nature gives me pain, but love makes me happy.

January 29, 1946

Life is not what people imagine. Man himself is not what people believe he is. Truth is not what the human mind imagines it to be.

I want to be sincere and open to the deepest fibers of my soul. At the first step into prison, I asked myself why I was imprisoned. In my social life, in my relations with the world in which I lived, I was always regarded as a very good person, an example of moral behavior. If I entered a conflict with anyone, it was only on behalf of truth. After much struggle, after much pain, when the cup of sufferings was full, a holy day came, in June 1943, when I fell with my face on the ground, kneeling, my forehead bowed, and having a humbled heart. I sobbed. I asked God to give me light. At that time I had lost all trust in people. I knew clearly that I was defending truth, so why was I suffering? Out of my soul that used to be full of enthusiasm, only love remained. Nobody could understand me.

In all my sobbing, I began to do prostrations. And all of a sudden—oh, Lord! How great are you, Lord!—I saw that my entire soul was filled with sins. I found the root of all human sins within me.

So many sins, and the eyes of my soul, hardened by pride, could not see them! How great God is!

When I saw all my sins, I felt the need to shout them out aloud, to cast them out from me. And a deep peace, a deep wave of light and love overfilled my heart. When the door was opened, I immediately came out from my cell and went to those who loved me the most and those who hated me and have wronged me the most. I confessed openly: "I am the most sinful human being. I do not deserve the trust of the basest human being. I am happy!"

Everyone was stunned. Some regarded me with disdain, others with indifference, and still others with a love that they themselves could not explain. Only one man told me, "You deserve to be kissed!" And I ran quickly to my cell, I crashed with my head on the pillow, and I continued to cry, thanking and glorifying God. ...

Since that day, I have consciously fought against sin. If you knew how difficult the war against sin is! I want you to know that I fought much against sin, not only here, in prison, but also when I was free. [Here, he confesses that, even if he was tempted physically, he did not fall, but he remained pure].[9]

In prison I examined my soul and I realized that, even if I had not sinned in deed, I had sinned in word and especially in thought. I went to the priest and,

9   The comments in brackets are those of Ioan Ianolide.

after a deep examination of my conscience, I made confession. My confession unburdened me.

And I still continue to fight. This fight does not end before death. Without repentance, no man can take a single step forward. The one who runs away from the reality of one's own soul is a liar. ... What is life? It is a gift from God so that we, people, cleanse ourselves from sin and prepare us, through Christ, for receiving eternal life. What is man? A being created out of God's boundless love, a being faced with the choice between happiness and death. ...

Be very careful! In social life, people judge others according to what they seem to be, and not according to what they truly are. Do not have illusions regarding any man—whoever does this will suffer bitterly —but love every man. Only one is perfect, only one is good, only one is pure: Christ God!

Now: what is truth? Truth is Christ, the Word of God. Try to enter Christ's presence sincerely and leave the world with its sins behind!

March 7, 1946

My beloved mother, I saw you in Norica's heart when she came to visit me in prison. You were good, gentle, and aware of everything that my soul experiences. I was silent and I was searching within me. I discovered Love there. ... Today I am so content! I look at my life and the world's life with peace, and I see the

Lord's work in everything. I look at your life, and I see a miracle of God.

My dear mother, I feel your presence so much! Tell me, mother, that you feel my love! Tell me, mother, that you feel I am at your side at all times! Tell me, mother, that you are happy! I want to tell you so much, mother! ... In the night, I wake up and I pray. I send all my thoughts to my mother, in the Făgăraş Country,[10] and there is so much peace inside me at that moment! And I can feel Tuţa, his boundless love. And I often think of the love between you and Tuţa. Such a beautiful home you created! And what a beautiful love!

Mother, I remember the summer days when I was a student in high school and I was walking with you in the garden, among the trees. And I remember the thoughts that you shared with me regarding my future. You desired to have a good daughter-in-law. I remember that I didn't think much about this. However, I was dreaming of having a wife, and I could see her in my imagination as a beautiful girl, whom I would love from the first moment I met her. I would love her with a unique love. ...

In those times past, the essence of my thoughts was to become a man of great value. What that meant

10 Făgăraş is a city in the center of Romania, at the foot of the Făgăraş Mountains. The region surrounding the city, including several villages, is called the Făgăraş country. At that time, Valeriu Gafencu's family lived in Făgăraş.

was to be a man who would play a key role in history, a man who would bring the greatest contribution to his nation. I wanted to do much good in the world. ... But man makes plans and God decides. Life continues to follow its stormy and great course for me. I ended up alone in Iași,[11] at the University. There I realized that great perspectives were opening for me indeed. I lived a normal life, and I was one of the most appreciated students, loved by everyone, and I had an unusual thirst for the Ideal: a new world, in which love and justice, perfect harmony, would reign.

In Iași, although my soul was thirsty for love, I did not tie my heart to any girl. Why? In my soul, I carried the image of a girl, my beloved, but I could never discover this girl embodied in any real creature. Thus, I continued to experience love in my own way, pouring it in all beings, but remaining with an empty spot in my heart, which needed to be filled.

But I was imprisoned. Was I sad then?... Was I happy?... I could not say. I could realize, though, with certainty that prison would solve a series of problems through suffering and separation from the world. I was fully convinced that I was suffering for truth. This brought a deep peace to my soul. I was on the way to accomplishing the Ideal.

11   Iași is one of the main cities of Romania, in the north-eastern part of the country, with reputable universities. It was the capital city of Moldova until 1859, when the principalities of Moldova and Wallachia were united and then formed Romania.

Dear mother, I would like you to know that I have suffered much. During the first winter, I used to wake up in the night and, in the solitude of the cell, in cold and hunger, I was contemplating darkness, whispering softly, so that only I could hear, but loudly enough for God to hear: "Mother, I am cold, I am hungry!"

At the beginning, it was tremendously difficult. But God was always with me. He did not leave me even for a moment. I began to confront the sufferings of the body, and I slowly began tasting of new joys. I saw that I am a sinful man. I shuddered because of my sins, because of my helplessness. I then realized that I, who had desired an ideal world with my whole heart, I was myself a sinful man. So I had to become a pure man first, a new man. And I began to fight the evil in me.

Slowly, the light of truth descended upon me. I began experiencing happiness in the midst of suffering. The emptiness I had in my heart, which I expected would be filled by the love of my beloved, was filled by Christ, the great Love. I then understood that truly great is the one who has a great love, that truly great is the one who sees himself as little.

Today I am happy. I love everyone through Christ. People understand and accept this path with so much difficulty! But I am convinced that this is the only path toward happiness. ...

May 15, 1946

We all search for happiness. We all desire it and try to find it. ... I go straight into the intimacy of your hearts and tell you: search for happiness in your souls. Do not look for it outside of yourselves. Do not wait for happiness to come from any other place than your inner being, your souls, where Christ dwells. If you wait for happiness from outside, you will experience deception after deception and will never reach it. I only tell you this: search for love and live it with humility! ... Whoever fulfills the word of Christ accomplishes the maximum, Everything!

May 15, 1946 (another letter)

Pay close attention and be careful in all things! A perfect legality and correctness. Prudence in every spoken or written word. These are very delicate times, and you may not perceive this. Have relationships with all people, but strictly within the framework of a Christian life. ...

Felix!...[12] Our souls met in a train, from Bucharest to Piatra Olt. We looked into each other's eyes, and a love made us friends for life. In him I saw a gigantic,

12   Editors note in the Romanian edition: "Second lieutenant Felix Guha, close friend of Valeriu Gafencu" (Ioan Ianolide, *Intoarcerea la Hristos*, 235).

titanic soul who lived under the weight of solitude. I do not feel worthy of his love. I can still not explain how we became friends: he is mature, with a vast culture, unusual knowledge, unique possibilities, and a high social status; I, on the other side, have nothing of what he has.

If he had lived today, Felix would have been totally transformed by the love I have for him and by the boundless trust he had in my sincerity. He would have reached the highest level of Christian experience. Having a Christian conscience, he would have become a man without peer.

May 19, 1946

I am happy. While my physical freedom is restricted by human laws, I was gifted with spiritual freedom through the mystery of love. This spiritual freedom is the most valuable good that I could have gained in this world filled with vanities. We serve our nation's salvation, our nation's spiritual renewal, only as long as we serve God.

May 28, 1946

There is much vanity on this earthly world, but the gifts God seeds in man's soul are so wonderful! Because of them, you accept the thought of death with joy—for death for Christ brings the happiness of eternal life. We will also rise, and, regardless of how small it is, any suffering that we have received with love, any sacrifice for God will weigh much at the hour of the feared Judgment. Then, on the Day of the Final Judgment, all our sins will be in the open, all the mistakes of our lives. This is why we must confess our sins to our spiritual father and to fight the good fight. Some will rise to life, but others to eternal punishment. Let us persevere in prayer, be watchful with humility and love, and believe in the mercy of God. ...

We spent this day as usual. In the evening, all three of us went for a walk.[13] We began to confess our spiritual states that we have lately experienced; it was a confession of sins. There were great moments, experienced with the full sincerity of our souls; there were confessions of the most delicate inner feelings and secrets. I feel that a life of pure cleanliness is asked of me, not only in word and deed, but also in thought and intentions.

We experience the fight with sin intensely. We desire the Resurrection in the depth of our souls. We are in a position that requires the utmost attention: we are on a knife-edge. For a long time, I have discerned and fought the subtlest thoughts that attempt

---

13   Editors note in the Romanian edition: "In the work colony at Galda, Valeriu Gafencu, Ioan Ianolide, and Marin Naidim formed a strong spiritual connection, based on mutual support in the difficult work of cleansing themselves of passions" (Ioan Ianolide, *Intoarcerea la Hristos,* 236).

to penetrate my soul. I realize that the devil tries to penetrate the soul by ways that seem innocent. ...

I search for humility, for it is very useful for the breaking of my heart. The fight against egoism is very difficult. I understand that a true man is the one who has succeeded in breaking self-love. I must fight against the tendency of solitude and, at the same time, I must fight against forming personal relationships that could bear the mark of egoism, in the sense that I must run away from the satisfaction that the soul experiences when it feels that others participate in its personal life and gifts.

Only one attitude is valid: a high Christian life of unceasing prayer. So, what you do must be clean—any work, thought, or word, any relationship, work, or rest, everything must be a state of prayer, of communion with God. Sin has been conquered by Love.

Fragments of undated letters sent from Galda between 1946 and 1948

I revel in the thought of total abandonment and permanent sacrifice. The Cross is dear to me. I also bear a cross. I feel the love of Christ the Savior, and I run to Him when temptations come over my passionate body. And the Lord helps me and gives me strength to overcome evil. How good God is!

Most of the time, I fight with my inner egoism. This is why solitude is dear to me. I love to listen to the whisper of the leaves and the murmur of the water. I am a free man. Christ has shattered the chains of my slavery!

Beloved brother,[14] never think that you are worthless. Wherever you are, you are there by the will of God and you have a certain purpose to fulfill. You will build your brother with your love and meekness. And you will reap great happiness. ... There is no sin that remains unpunished. However, if you repent sincerely and you pray to God with a broken heart, He will forgive you and will send you His grace. From the other side, there is no good deed, no good thought, regardless of how simple it may be, that is not rewarded. Be, however, humble, for it is not you, but God who works through you.

I hear titmice singing. How simple they are![15]

The owner of the vineyard just came here. He has sunglasses. When I saw him, I remembered that I am an inmate who works on his domain. This thought humbles me. But God sends me great joy. I work on God's earth. People are proud and do not want to see that only One is master of all: Christ!

---

14   Valeriu Gafencu did not have brothers. The letter is probably addressed to a friend.
15   The titmouse is a small woodland bird.

Oh, Lord! How can people judge and condemn their brethren to death, before God judged them?

I look into my soul. There is great serenity. Over the water, slowly, a gentle wave trembles and is lost in immensity. There are temptations which, however, do not succeed in disturbing my peace. I do not allow them to penetrate deeply. I fight them. "And the Spirit of the Lord hovered over the waters."[16] How great are you, Lord!

Now, I am with my thought in a monastery!

I am a small, helpless man who has no good works. This is who I am in reality.

When I was a child, I used to love pigeons very much. However, as with all desires, I could not have them for long. I understand today that it was God's love, which was taking from me the joys of this world so that I learn, by renunciation, to love purely, perfectly. I still love pigeons today, but I no longer feel my soul tied to them; I love them through God. And I understand that God's love will never leave me. He will intervene in my life at any time I will tie my soul to a human joy or love. He will either help me to pull me out of it, or He will take it from me; He will give me instead the freedom of my soul, which is the greatest good.

16 See Gen 1.2.

I am happy, serene, and confident in the destiny of my life. God has always helped me. I am ready for anything.

Mama was a simple girl, who had finished elementary school and had no other wealth than the virginity of her soul and body. Tuţa was a good man, healthy, strong, with a beautiful past, a student at the Polytechnic Institute, and well regarded by all people of value who lived in Bessarabia in those times. They loved one another. ... I see Tuţa sobbing, trembling out of love and pain: his son, Valeriu, has left. And I am so sinful!

The desire to ascend to heaven can be seen in all nature. The mountain, the trees, the larks, the vulture, and the soul of man are eternally thirsting to go higher and higher, closer to the Lord, further away from this world.

I miss a peaceful, far-away place, a hut or a hovel dug in stone, a cell at the foot of a mountain, where I could be like the birds of the sky, surrounded by friendly nature and having the Lord Jesus eternally in my soul. I would humbly love in peace, forgotten by the world. At times, I think about becoming a priest, but I am not worthy of it. I look at the earth. One day, I will also be earth, and others will stir up the dust. My body will become smithereens and smoke. From my body, another life will probably grow. My soul will be in heaven, where it will wait for its judgment. I desire to be saved.

I hear the lark singing in the park. The nightingales are singing. They are dear to me. I fight the sinful thoughts that try to enter my heart. There is peace in my soul.

Other Letters

January 31, 1948

In all circumstances, pray to God that His will be done. I see God's work in your souls. I see His care for you and I am so content!

Love is the greatest virtue. Love is actually perfection. When you give love to this earthly world instead of gifting love to the Spring of all that is good, to God and, by Him, to your neighbor, you change its meaning, and love is transformed from the most wonderful virtue into the most dangerous passion.

God bestowed on man so many gifts that, by persevering in virtue, with the help of the Heavenly Father, we can be saved. God gave man so many talents that, by them, he could fight, draw closer to Him, give himself, and sacrifice himself. If we do not use the "talent" entrusted to us, we are slaves of sin.

Thus, the problem of using the talents gifted by

God is real for every one of us. We are not allowed to use the talent for evil or to bury it in the earth. "Your own of your own, we offer unto you, on behalf of all and for all."[17] Let us offer to God what He gave us. He gave us life, so let us live for Him. He gave us love, so let us offer it to Him.

We pay in this life and in the eternal life. In this life, expiation by suffering has two aspects: a saving role and a cleansing role. In the eternal life, expiation by suffering is eternal torment. This is why it is proper to thank the Lord when he punishes us here, in this life. So let us be very careful in how we use God's gift.

March 7, 1948

I follow each and all of you with my love and prayer. Even if I am far from you in body, I am not so in spirit, for I am always with you.

Undated Letters

When I see you saddened, I take your hand and tell you: Keep your chin up! Forward! Courage! Any true joy is gained at the price of a sacrifice. Any citadel is conquered with faith, manliness, boldness, trust in the mission given by God, and especially prayer.

---

17   These are the words the priest says during Liturgy at the moment of the elevation of the Gifts.

Walk on the thorny path, by the sufferings experienced by a Christian who loves truth. ...

I want you to know that I consider these times a trial and I perceive them as a state of expiation: my soul is serene and filled with peace, and I have a mysterious joy and much hope. I want you to know that I am happy. These times are for the confirmation of the path that I confessed years and years ago. This is such a deep joy that I can say that I look at death with much inner peace and with the hope of the future life

I wish to have many days so that I could prepare for it, with God's help. I give you all the love of my soul.

Poems

Dar

Frate dragă, din grădină
Îţi trimit în dar un crin,
Să-ţi mângâie blând privirea
Cu veşmântul lui virgin.

Floare dalbă, floare albă,
Cât de mult aş da şi eu,
Îmbrăcat în haina-ţi albă,
Să mă duc la Dumnezeu.

Răsădit acolo sus,
În grădina minunată,
Să-mi simt viaţa-mbălsămată
Cu iubirea lui Iisus.

Plâng înăbuşit în noapte
Şi suspin cu glasul stins:
Dă-mi veşmântul alb de Nuntă,
Cu crini minunaţi încins!

A Gift

As a gift I send a lily,
Dear brother, from the garden.
It would give your eyes some comfort
With its pure, virginal garment.

Dear white, beloved flower,
How I'd wish that I could go
All embraced by your clean costume
To my Father, white as snow.

Seedling thus would I become,
In the most wonderful garden,
And my life would have as warden
Jesus' love, from where I come.

In the night I cry all muffled
And I sigh with my faint voice:
Give to me the wedding garment
With white lilies; I rejoice.

Dor

Trăiesc flămând, trăiesc o bucurie
frumoasă ca un crin din paradis.
Potirul florii e mereu deschis
şi-i plin cu lacrimi şi cu apă vie.
Potirul florii e o-mpărăţie.

Când răii mă defaimă şi mă-njură
şi-n clocot de mânie ura-şi varsă,
potirul lacrimilor se revarsă
şi-mi primeneşte sufletul de zgură.
Atunci Iisus de mine mult se-ndură.

Sub crucea grea ce mă apasă sânger,
cu trupu-ncovoiat de neputinţă.
Din când în când, din cer coboar-un înger
şi sufletul mi-l umple cu credinţă.
M-apropii tot mai mult de biruinţă.

Dor[1]

I live in hunger, in great joy I live
A joy as a divine lily in heaven.
The chalice of the flower is always open
And filled with living water and with tears.
The flower's chalice is the kingdom I live.

When evil ones abuse and denigrate me,
My body burning with their boiling hatred,
The chalice of the tears, oh, how sacred,
Renews my soul all dry and slaggy.
I am embraced with Jesus Christ's great mercy.

I bleed under the cross that presses me;
My body's crooked, and I am quite helpless.
From time to time an angel comes and blesses
And fills my soul with faith. No longer weary,
The triumph I approach: Jesus wins in me.

---

[1] The title has been preserved in Romanian due to the difficulty in finding a suitable translation. Bishop Bartolomeu Anania said about *dor*: "*Dor* has always a purpose, a direction; it goes somewhere. ... You have *dor* for someone you had and you lost, or for someone who is far away. [...] The *dor* attracts you, it attempts to fill a spiritual emptiness, and it is always expressed ineffably, so it cannot be placed into words." I think the best rendering in English is "longing."

Mă plouă-n taină razele de soare,
m-adapă Iisus cu apă vie,
grăuntele zvârlit în groapă-nvie,
cu viaţa îmbrăcată-n sărbătoare:
Trăiesc flămând, trăiesc o bucurie.

Refren:
Sub flacăra iubirii arzătoare,
din zori de zi şi până-n noapte-aştept.
Te chem şi noaptea, ghemuit cu capu-n piept:
Iisuse, Iisuse!
Încet mă mistui, ca o lumânare.

The sunshine rains on me in secret, ardent.
To drink from living water Jesus gives me.
The seed thrown in the tomb again can live
With its life fully dressed in wedding garment.
I live in hunger, in great joy I live.

Refrain:
Under the flame of burning love—my mantle,
I wait from dawn to night to be your conquest.
Even in night I call on you, head fallen on my chest:
Jesus, Jesus!
I slowly melt, a burning candle.

Poezie

Mi-s ochii trişti şi fruntea obosită
de-atâta priveghere şi-aşteptare,
mi-e inima bolnavă, istovită
de grea şi îndelungă alergare
şi plânge ca o pasăre rănită.

Când ochii mi-i închid şi cat in mine
puteri să urc Golgota până sus,
o voce, un ecou din adâncime
îmi spune blând: "Viaţa e Iisus!
Mărgăritarul preţios e-n tine."

Privesc la dimineaţa minunată
a Învierii Tale din Mormânt,
cu Magdalena, ca şi altădată,
îngenunchez 'naintea Ta, plângând;
şi-s fericit şi plâng cu Tine-n gând.

A Poem

My eyes are sorrow and my head is tired
By so much watchfulness and so much waiting,
My heart is sick, I feel my health required
By long and heavy running—it's unending:
An injured bird—my heart is still on fire.

And when my eyes are closed, I search within me
For strength, Golgotha I have to ascend,
And from my depth, a voice, an echo, tells me:
"Remember: Life is Jesus!" I consent.
"The precious pearl is in you." A guarantee.

I contemplate the otherworldly morning
When you, alive, rose from the tomb; I do,
Again, with Magdalene, answer the calling
And so I kneel before you, crying, too:
I'm happy and I cry beholding you.

Mina

Un gând smerit şi simplu, o lumină,
Spre Tine se înalţă lin din mină
Şi sufletul înlăcrimat se roagă:
"O, vino, de păcate mă dezleagă!
Pe fruntea mea senină mâna-Ţi pune
Şi cheamă-mă încetişor pe nume,
Cum Ţi-ai chemat prietenul din groapă;
Te rog, Iisuse, dă-mi un pic de apă!

Dă-mi Pâine, Apă vie dă-mi din Viţă,
Să simt pulsând viaţa în mlădiţă,
Din mila Ta, dă-mi inimă curată
Şi faţa Ta divină Ţi-o arată
În ceasul fericitei mele despărţiri
De lumea asprei noastre pribegiri.

Iisuse Doamne, vino-n zori,
Te cheamă cei din închisori,
O, vino, mina luminează,
Pe noi ne binecuvântează!"

The Mine

A humble, simple thought—a gladsome light
From our mine rises to you in flight;
A soul that bathes in tears slowly prays:
"Oh, come, so that my sins from me you raise!
Then on my tranquil forehead place your hand
And gently call my name toward your land,
Just as you called your friend out of the grave;
Oh, Jesus, give me water, please, I pray!

And Bread, and living Water from the Vine,
To feel life in my branches as a sign;
And in your mercy, give me a clean heart
The hour when I joyfully depart
From our world of bitter wandering;
Make me a witness of your face shining.

Jesus, Lord, to us please come at dawn,
Prisoners call you before they're gone.
Oh, come, and to this mine give light,
And bless us all with all your might!"

Imn

Vă cheamă Domnul Slavei la lumină,
Vă cheamă mucenicii-n veşnicii,
Fortificaţi Biserica Creştină
Cu pietre vii, zidite-n temelii!

Să crească-n inimile voastre-nfrânte
Un om născut din nou, armonios,
Pe chipurile voastre să se-mplânte
Pecetea Domnului Iisus Hristos.

Un clopot tainic miezul nopţii bate,
Iisus coboară pe pământ,
Din piepturile voastre-nsângerate
Răsună imnul Învierii sfânt.

Smulgeţi-vă din ceata celor răi,
Intraţi în cinul oastei creştineşti,
Priviţi spre Porţile Împărăteşti,
Căci cei din urmă fi-vor cei dintâi.

Veniţi creştini, luaţi Lumină,
Cu sufletul senin, purificat,
Veniţi flămânzi, gustaţi din cină,
E Nunta Fiului de Împărat!

Hymn

Our Lord of Glory calls you to the light,
And to eternity the martyrs call you,
To fortify the Church you all must fight
So you become its living stones, all new!

A new, harmonious man, fully rebuilt,
Should start increasing in your broken hearts,
And on your faces, you should have instilled
The seal of Lord and Master Jesus Christ.

At midnight, mystically, you hear bell sounds;
To be on earth, Jesus descends,
And from your bleeding chests a hymn resounds:
The holy hymn of resurrection, friends.

Come out of the horde of those wicked;
Enroll in the ranks of the Christian army!
Behold the gates of our holy kingdom,
Remember, the ones who are last the first will be.

Oh, come, you Christians, take the light,
With gentle souls approach, don't shun!
Come hungry, taste the supper in delight!
It is the wedding of the King's only Son!

Rămas-bun

Sângerând de răni adânci,
De zile fără soare,
De răni ascunse şi puroi,
Cu oasele slabe şi moi,
Stau ghemuit în pat şi mă gândesc
Că în curând am să vă părăsesc,
Prieteni dragi!

Nu plângeţi că mă duc de lângă voi,
Şi c-o să fiu zvârlit ca un gunoi,
Cu hoţii în acelaşi cimitir;
Căci crezul pentru care m-am jertfit
Cerea o viaţă grea şi-o moarte de martir.

Luându-L pe Iisus de Împărat,
Năvalnic am intrat pe poarta strâmtă,
Luându-mă cu diavolul la trântă.
Şi ani de-a rându-ntr-una m-am luptat
Să devin altul,
Un erou,
Om nou.

Şi-am vrut
Neamul să-l mut
De-aici, de jos,
La Domnul Iisus Hristos.

Farewell

Bleeding out from wounds so deep,
From gloomy, sunless days,
From hidden wounds, with bones so weak,
Buried in pus always,
I'm crouching in my bed. An adieu,
I think, I'll tell to all of you,
My dear friends!

Cry not that I depart from you,
That they will throw me like a piece of trash
Within a tomb where thieves will be my crew.
The creed for which I'll give my final breath
Asked for a hard life and a martyr's death.

With Jesus as my Lord and King,
I rushed through the narrow gate, entered the ring,
And with the devil I began to fight.
And I did fight all years, day and night,
So that I become another,
A champion,
A new man.

And I desired,
By this thought I was fired,
To take my people in flight
To our Lord Jesus Christ.

Acum, când văd cât sunt de păcătos,
De mic şi de neputincios,
Că am nevoie multă de-ndurare,
De dragoste, de milă, de iertare,
Că numai Dumnezeu le poate toate
Şi lumea din robie El o scoate,
Devin copil supus,
Sunt umilit
Şi-s fericit.

Din cerul Tău înalt şi prea-ales,
Părinte, când mă vei lua la Tine,
Prietenilor mei de pe pământ
Redă-le Tu, în alb veşmânt,
Un suflet care i-a iubit şi i-a'nţeles.

[*lipseşte ultima strofă*]

Now, when I see that I am so sinful, that I crawl,
That I'm so helpless and so small,
That I need mercy in my illness,
And love, compassion, much forgiveness,
That only God can do all things,
Can change man's shackles into wings,
I too become a meek, small boy,
I'm humbled,
And in my heart there's joy.

From your high, eternal heaven,
My Father, when you take me up to you,
Remember all my friends here on earth:
Give back to them, dressed all in white,
A soul that loved and understood them, too.

[*the last stanza is missing*]

Colind

Pe malul Trotuşului
Cântă robii Domnului,
Înjugaţi la jugul Lui.

Dar cântarea lor e mută,
Că-i din suferinţă multă
Şi-i cu lacrimi împletită.

În inima robului,
Domnu-Şi face ieslea Lui,
În noaptea Crăciunului.

Flori de crin din ceruri plouă
Peste ieslea Lui cea nouă
Şi din flori picură rouă.

Stă un copilaş în zare
Şi priveşte cu mirare
La fereastra de-nchisoare.

Lângă micul copilaş
S-a oprit un îngeraş,
Ce-i şopteşte drăgălaş:

Carol

On the bank of the Trotush,
The Lord's servants his yoke push,
And they sing, and push... and push...

Their singing is slow, silent
For their suffering is violent
And their hearts with tears vibrant.

In the humble servant's heart
The Lord makes his manger: light
On this peaceful Christmas night.

From heavens it rains with lilies;
All of them his manger seizes,
Dew from flowers feels like breezes.

At the horizon, a small child
Looks at us, his gaze is wild:
In prison we are exiled.

But an angel comes to him.
Seeing that his eyes get dim
He sings gracefully a hymn:

"Azi Crăciunul s-a mutat
Din palat la închisoare,
Unde-i Domnu-ntemnițat."

Şi copilul cel din zare
A venit la închisoare
Să trăiască praznic mare.

Refrain:
Lăsaţi-i pe copii să vină,
Să-mi aducă din grădină
Dalbe flori de sărbători,
Dalbe, dalbe flori!

"Today, Christmas has arisen
Not in a palace, but in prison,
For the Lord has been imprisoned."

So the child from the far east
Comes to us, his soul released,
To rejoice in the great feast.

Refrain:
Let the children come to me.
From the garden, they bring flowers:
Flowers—flowers for the feasts—
White, white flowers.

O stea călătoare de la Răsărit

O stea călătoare de la Răsărit,
Cu razele albe de-argint,
Lunecă înspre albastrul senin
Al cerului viu înflorit.
Şi steaua-L vesteşte pe Pruncul Mesia
Născut din Fecioara Maria.
Un miel bland se uită şi-ar vrea să- sărute
Pe pruncul scăldat în lumină.
În noaptea Crăciunului alb şi senin
O Mamă cu Pruncul la sân,
Curată-n iubire, priveşte-n uimire
Plinindu-se Bunavestire.
Un Prunc Sfânt se naşte în noaptea-nstelată
Din Sfânta Fecioară şi Duhul cel Sfânt;
Al Tatălui drept Cuvânt
Coboară azi pe pământ
Făclie pe veci luminată!

The Star from the East[2]

The Star from the East,
With radiant beams of silver,
Slides into the clear blue
Of the sky that is in bloom.
The star brings the tidings of the child Messiah
Born of the Virgin Mary.
A meek lamb approached and would like to embrace
The babe who is bathed in light.
On the night of Christmas, white and serene,
A mother pure in love holds dear her child
And beholds in wonder
How the Annunciation comes to pass.
A holy babe is born on this starlit night
From the holy Virgin and the Holy Spirit;
The Father's Word
Descends to earth:
A light eternally lit!

2   The title has been added as the author did not attach a title.

Dialogues

On Monasticism

I DISCOVERED Christ and I have desired to follow him on the narrowest path, out of an inner need to give myself fully and out of the conviction that the world can be saved only through Christ. I have not left the world, but I have left everything that was worldly in me for the world's sake. I did not give up life by desiring to become a monk, but I wanted to serve life in a higher form.

The highest attribute of monasticism is not virginity or asceticism, but a spirit enlightened by grace for ministry toward life. A monk prays for people. A monk's aversion to the world must be understood as an ascetic method, because monasticism is an exceptional life, a life against life for the sake of life. The monks are the fools that defy even nature in order to unite themselves to Christ and serve people. Their virginity is the expression of purity, and the passion-filled world needs this. The physiological effect of chastity becomes a spring of spiritual power, but not for a personal purpose, as some believe, but for a communal purpose, as the Lord teaches us. Monasticism is the superior path of preparation for the world, because the world needs fools for holy things so that it is made holy.

We currently live in an era when Christians discover another path of confession: the folly of the Cross, of sacrifice for Truth. Christ's enemies have unleashed the greatest and cruelest persecution against Christians. Now, whoever believes has to be ready for death. This path is a spiritual privilege of great beauty, out of which monasticism itself comes up with new values and meanings.

Thus, I thought it was necessary to take the monastic vow, even if we are on the path of martyrdom. When you are faced with giving up your life, the rough monastic vows remain far away, but they have value because they demonstrate the zeal for holy things; when faith is confessed with the price of humility and tortures, all ascetic toils seem easy, but receiving them demonstrates the spiritual direction of the sacrifice. Thus, now, when I find myself in the situation of giving up my life for faith, my monastic vow is a consolation for my soul, even if the vow is not put into practice.

Monasticism appeared in the history of Christianity when the Church became official and the faithful who were filled with ardor were not content with the mode of life of the Christian society at that time, and so they withdrew to live the Gospel authentically. They constituted true centers of Christian spirituality and they much influenced medieval Christianity and even in the modern era. It is well known that monasteries have played a major cultural role, that they had a brilliant educational role, a social role in charity, and a role in the preaching of Christianity. Through men filled with Spirit, the monasteries often influenced politics and history, even if they did not always succeed in raising them to the level of Christian conscience.

Today, however, Satan is worried that he would lose his power over the world. This is why he is on a full offensive against Christians, monastics and the laity. Monasticism is discredited by false, ill-intentioned slogans. The devil tempts today's Christians, as he tempted the Lord in the mountain, to be just like him, and when they refuse it, he applies the method of exterminating them through all means. Some come to buy us with gold, others come to cut

us with the sword, but we go deeper into the spirit of
the Gospel.

We need people, monks and the laity, who confess
and live as Christians. We do not withdraw from the
battle of history, but we are shaped and we become
strong in its bitter tension. All the power in heaven
and on earth was entrusted to Christ. The tortures
to which we are submitted are doors through which
Christ freshens the Church and the world over and
over again and raises them higher and higher.

On Priesthood

Q. Do you believe, Valeriu, that celibate priesthood
is a good thing?

A. From the point of view of dedication, it is good,
because the celibate facilitates the detachment
from any human interest and connection; however, it is very difficult to observe the celibate, and
thus it is a great temptation. The orthodox formula seems to be wisest: monastic hierarchs and
priests with families.

Q. However, doesn't this formula of a family priesthood have its own shortcomings?

A. Ideally, the priest, if he has a family, must be able
to get away from it for Christ, and if he has material goods, he must be as if he did not have them.
In order to be alive for Christ, the priest must be

dead to the world—but precisely in order to serve the world. He must first be an example of Christian living. The priests must let the world of sin bury their own dead, while they have to snatch people from it to build the Christian world. It would be good if the material problems of the priests' families were taken over and integrated by the community. We must reject the bourgeois theory of the *kulak* priest.

Q. Should the priests and hierarchs enter into politics?

A. The priest is the spiritual guide of Christianity, but he is interested in the problems of the entire humanity, so he is engaged in all human problems, and that much more those which give orientation to the world. So, if politics means orientation, the priest deals with orientation. Taking into consideration the imperfection of human condition, in which forms are continually changing, the priests do not govern, but they rather keep watch over governments; they keep watch over the good, and so they are fixed on a spiritual, moral, and ideological plan. The clergy must maintain its freedom and independence from the political realm in order to be able to influence it and, eventually, refresh it. But letting the world be governed by chance means losing its clerical mission. The ideal society is the one led by the divine-human cooperation, clerical and laity, by the cooperation between church and state. The clergy has the difficult mission to form the spirituality that gives the background to the unfolding of history.

Q. In which fields can the clergy work directly?

A. First, the domain of the sacred is reserved for it. All Christians have grace, but only the priests can administer it. Second, they have the word, through all of its forms of expression: utterance, sound, movement, color, and imagery. Thus, the clergy can work in education, philosophy, poetry, art, music, journalism, science, sociology, and economy. At the same time, they are also called to think politically and to express themselves on political problems, but this depends on historical circumstances. At times, Christians have rejected certain governments, other times they accepted them without appropriating them, and, when they could, they gave expression to their own governments. Often, though, these governments are Christian in form, but without Christian content, because political forces succeeded in defeating the Christian perspective. We remind here the fight of Saint John Chrysostom with Emperor Arcadius and the slavery that was practiced within the Christian world.

Q. If Christianity brought the idea of equality among people, why is there a church hierarchy?

A. As unique beings, all people are equal before

God. We are also equal before justice, the right to life, the right of expression, but we manifest our diversity precisely through expression. In creation—so ontologically, naturally—we are different. Equality among people does not lead to uniformity, but to hierarchy; the problem is not eliminating the hierarchy of values, but establishing a healthy criterion for hierarchy. The world itself is created hierarchically. The angels are also placed hierarchically. People, then, also stand on hierarchical levels, according to their gifts and their worth. Spiritual life itself goes through hierarchical stages toward perfection. Satan, in his hell, knows hierarchy, and evil people are ranked in their evilness. Contrary to the hierarchy of evil, pride, passions, and egoism, Christians bring the hierarchy of good, virtues, meekness, and love. The church hierarchy has three levels of investment, but they also need to be levels of experience; otherwise, we run the risk of introducing the model of the hierarchy of evil in the hierarchy of good, under a Christian mask. In principle, then, there is no conflict between equality and hierarchy among people.

On Mysticism

Q. Valeriu, the notion of *mysticism* is denigrated today; however, people believe in God and need communion with him. You yourself have a powerful inner experience. What should then be done?

A. First, we must reveal the bad faith of those who have succeeded, here and in other places, to discredit the notion of mysticism. Mysticism will remain at the center of the Christian rebirth that is being prefigured, because Christians enter into communion with Christ through it, in a gradual spiritual process of cleansing and perfection. It begins with man's reorientation toward himself in order to search for Christ and to arrive at union with God through Love. Inner experience changes nature and transforms man into a bearer of Christ. Unlike morality, which imposes the rigor of commandments, mysticism is a real, intimate act of living in the Holy Spirit. Being an 'art,' it presupposes a guide, an adviser. This is an Abba, a Father, who, beyond the fact that he administers grace, has himself an inner life and hesychast practice.

Q. What is the beginning of inner life with Christ?

A. Faith, faith in God. There are people who believe due to their nature and to the environment in which they lived. There are people who reach faith from within themselves and after searches and wanderings. There are people who pervert their faith in foreign, degrading, and even satanic manifestations. Faith is a potential component of the soul's structure, but it necessitates an attentive and organized process of knowledge. The Church has the role of teaching us the right faith.

Q. If the beginning of inner life is faith, what is its end, its crowning?

A. Faith is a small seed which grows continually in this life and in the future life, until the perfection of man and his union with God through love. Love is, then, the highest virtue, which does not replace faith, but strengthens it.

On the "Medievalism" of Christianity

A politician with liberal[1] convictions told Valeriu:

For me, faith is an institution that we have to encourage as a corrective for human egoism and abuses. Beyond its socio-political role, it presents no interest to me. A politician does not need God. Faith must be restricted politically in order to avoid a new obscurantist Middle Age.

Valeriu answered:

Sir, for someone like you, suffering is soul-saving. By suffering you will arrive at the light of faith.

---

1   After communism came into power, historical parties were outlawed and their important members were imprisoned. The liberals were members of the National Liberal Party; its doctrine was based in the classical liberalism of the 19th century.

You will then understand that you are small and imperfect, that your light is darkness, that you can be a true man only through God, that the horizons of knowledge are opened only through faith, and, finally, that the world cannot be redeemed without faith. You are the herald of a preconceived idea about the Middle Ages and of a falsification of Christianity. More than anyone else, a politician should be faithful because, by directing the world, he fulfills God's will, and he thus has great responsibilities. As for the Church and her role as institution, she is not a corrective, but an integration of the world in Christ; she is not preoccupied with a part, but with the whole. Since you did not want to receive faith because of materialist egoism, suffering and death come to you through materialism egoism. Bourgeois egoism is crushed by its more terrible son, the atheist-materialist vanity. I hope from all my heart that you reach faith prior to death, but this would mean to follow Christ."

That man came to faith.

On Peace

Q. Valeriu, what is peace?

A. Peace is a mystery and it can only be found in Christ, through Christ, and for Christ.

Q. Is peace in people's souls or in the world, in history or in eternity?"

A. Being in Christ, it is in all and through all.

Q. Can there be a false inner peace?

A. Passions lead to a state of addiction which becomes permanent, but it is not peace; errors also lead to a false state that claims to be all knowing, but a moment of truth comes, and such a state proves to be false peace; the evil spirit can diabolize man to blindness, but this is not peace, but slavery; the ego, vanity, the tendency of domination may deceive us by a personal peace, deprived of God, but man will certainly discover that he is a creature and that he can only find peace in God.

Q. Can there be inner peace without the unseen war?

A. If someone does not fight and does not conquer passions and ignorance, he does not know peace.

Q. What is the unseen war?

A. Return within yourself and you will see!

Q. Can there be inner peace without peace with people?

A. As long as you are guilty before people, willingly or unwillingly, knowingly or unknowingly, by omission or action, you cannot be at peace with God or with yourself.

Q. What is inner peace in Christ?

A. It is life in the Spirit of Truth, the kingdom of the Holy Spirit in man. It requires discernment among spirits and the capacity of steadfastness in Truth.

Q. It seems that it is difficult to delineate good from evil.

A. This is why man is man, free man, and king; man is such that he can discern among spirits. If we have no discernment, we are not worthy to be humans. Humans must be saints."

Q. Is peace in the Law or in Grace?

A. In Grace!

Q. Peace, in people's hearts as in the world, seems to be totally unstable!

A. People's peace depends on the measure in which they find themselves in the Spirit of Truth, so it is a spiritual problem first, even it if manifested politically, socially, economically, culturally, educationally, or morally. All people's problems are problems of conscience, and conscience can only find peace within the religious realm. The religious is fundamental in history.

Q. Valeriu, is peace determined by conscience or by power?

A. It is a mistake to accept the peace of power without truth. The peace of slavery cannot be accepted! The peace of evil cannot be accepted! Satan offers you his power if you bow to him, but all power in heaven and on earth was given to Christ, so Christians cannot accept the tempting peace of Satan.

Q. Valeriu, is peace a struggle?

A. Peace springs from the victory of the good over evil, either at the level of conscience or at the level of history. You find here the meaning of the unseen war of the ascetics and the apocalyptic meaning of history.

Q. So should peace be on the offensive unceasingly?

A. Peace must be on the offensive and always watchful. God's peace descended through the "offensive" of the incarnation of our Lord Christ and by the "offensive" of the Holy Spirit, who will work in the world until His second coming. Christianity is expression, search, daring, labor, fight, and power of sacrifice. Christians will only accept Christ's peace, regardless of how many sacrifices it will require of them.

Q. Must peace be protected?

A. Some people protect God's peace, others Satan's peace. However, the power of the apocalyptic beast will be destroyed by the power of the Lamb.

Q. What are the Christian methods of battle?

A. In the fight for affirmation, Christianity is spiritual and thus free. In defense, Christians are often obligated to answer to the aggressor with his weapons: David had to kill Goliath, St. Nestor threw Lyaeus in spears and received martyrdom.

Q. Are we for peace or for war?

A. There is a peace more destructive than any war, and there is a war that brings peace. Look into the spirit that gives birth to the events and the finality which they pursue, and you will then know what to do.

Q. We always hear talk about peace!

A. Each power proposes its own peace, but they are all hypocrites, masking their own domination under the vague notion of peace.

Q. What does today's Christian world miss: faith, truth, or power?

A. First, it is a crisis of faith; on this background, the world places itself outside of truth, and this is why God has taken the power from Christians' hands.

Q. How should we interpret the satanic power[2] of our century?

A. Beyond historical explanations, there are some structural explanations and, when all is told, spiritual ones. This world's structures are atheist-materialist, and the forces born in the East tend to shatter the planet. People are so much possessed by power, matter, and pleasure that they live in a hallucinating way. The disaster is imminent, either by peaceful or military means, due to the evil spirit which masters the way of life of the modern world. The world needs suffering in order to reorient itself spiritually. God has His own ways of intervening in history. We do not participate in this disaster, but we are under its destroying wave, because we confess Truth before

2   "The satanic power" designates communism.

people. However, today's people cannot receive it, because they are once again the sons of Satan."

On Freedom

Q. Is freedom an emanation from the evil?

A. Not at all. Evil does not exist ontologically. There is no evil in God. Evil is a misinterpretation of the freedom with which the Creator gifted people and angels, His creatures who have free conscience. Evil begins with Satan's pride and man's disobedience.

Q. Does God respect man's freedom?

A. By his omniscience, God respected man's freedom ontologically, because he foresaw the birth of his Son in creation; by his omni-benevolence, God made man and he suffers together with us until the world is saved. Man's nature is free, but there is no absolute freedom in creation, but only in the Creator.

Q. Does Satan respect man's freedom?

A. Satan does not know the inner part of man, but he uses all tools to enslave man, because Satan is a worthless slave himself. There is no freedom in evil.

Q. Does man respect man's freedom?

A. By egoism and desire to dominate, man is a wolf for man; by virtue and enlightening of grace, man is Christ for man. Man's respect for man is an issue having to do with men's deification.

Q. What is man's freedom?

A. Man must free himself from the tyranny of sin, the tyranny of nature, the tyranny of his neighbors, the tyranny of ignorance, and, after all, to conquer death. These things can be accomplished only through Christ.

Q. But what is slavery?"

A. It is the opposite of emancipation, so the slavery to passions, to the laws of nature, to man, to ignorance, and, in the last phase, the slavery of death.

Q. Is it possible to give freedom to evil?

A. Evil has freedom, but people must protect their freedom, their dignity, their integrity, their values, and their faith. The freedom that evil possesses is not also justification for governing; it must be challenged and eliminated from the world.

Q. Can there be false freedom?

A. If there can be a false christ, a false freedom can also naturally exist. It can be spiritual, political, or social. All the forms of manifestation of freedom are valuable only in Truth.

Q. What is the rapport between freedom and authority?

A. In our world, there cannot be freedom without authority, nor authority without freedom. Here, they are in an unstable balance, but they are absolute only in God.

Q. What are the main criteria of a free conscience?

A. First, there are God's commandments, then the natural and vital necessities, and then the values that have been consecrated by human experience and the law established by people—but all of these must be redefined and understood within context.

Q. Which is the authority that gives freedom weight?

A. It is obvious that man is not the creator and master of the world and of life, that man alone does not have the right to be a master of people. Only the man who is in continual communion with God, the godly man, has dominion over the world and enters into universal community.

Q. Since we are free and imperfect people, how do you see the problem of man's infallibility?

A. At the level of personal conscience, man is infallible by the personal certitude of truth, but with the exception that he is deprived exactly of infallibility. Man alone cannot be infallible. Only Christ was an infallible Man.

Q. What is then man's freedom?

A. It is the medium within which human personality is developed, it is the condition of human responsibility, and it also is the justification of the man-king.

Q. What is the difference between freedom and freedoms?

A. Freedom is the condition of man, while freedoms

are rights. Freedoms define and also limit freedom. Freedom is in spirit, while freedoms are in letter.

Q. What is the condition of the universe in rapport with man?

A. The universe and nature were conceived to correspond to the freedom of man. It is an astonishing equilibrium among multiple forces. Man's material universe functions the same way as man's spiritual universe, and both lead man to God.

Q. Can man determine his own destiny?

A. The materialist atheists, who are obsessed by pleasures, by the desire of domination and by egoism, have created modern civilization, which culminates in technicality. They have isolated human nature and left behind God's commandments. Their attempt to create an earthly and sensual heaven has, however, failed. Nature is exhausted and polluted, becoming inappropriate for life. At its turn, the technologies have more capacities for destruction than for construction. To all of these, we can add the worse of all evils: humans' alienation. In these conditions, the advocates of modern anthropocentrism no longer feel masters of the destinies of the world which they have created themselves. Thus, the alienated world, without God, finds the punishment for its own evilness.

Q. What is freedom in the vision of atheist materialism?

A. A farce, a kind of manifestation of the lying christ. Materialist determinism culminates in the conditioning of conscience as a complex of conditioned reflexes by which man is finished as man, as personality, because he no longer has freedom and no longer has holiness in him.

Q. However, atheist materialism uses strong ideas, such as freedom, communism, equality, justice, matter, people, science, etc.

A. The spirit and vision of atheist materialism pervert all values, because they place them in the service of egoism and tyranny. It is the proof that human values are not absolute by themselves, but they have worth depending on the spirit, the sense, and the measure with which they are used. Everything is true, good, and useful in Christ only. Outside of him, everything is disaster.

Q. How can man find his fulfillment?

A. Man's fulfillment is in his communion with the Holy Spirit. The Holy Spirit is called to bring unity in diversity, to bring order in history, holiness in life. Holiness is not something seraphic, unearthly, and esoteric, but it is the opening that Christ makes toward a world lived in the Holy Spirit.

Q. Will the Christian world of the 20th century receive the vision of creative and Messianic freedom?

A. The tragic events through which modern world

goes will create the conditions for the return to faith. We must come back to the Holy Spirit, the Gospel, and the apostolic strength. We have the duty to shout with our whole being the Truth, the repentance, and the world's return to God. Christianity is reborn in the fiery ovens filled with tortures that the atheist materialism owns. Satan will lose the world that he believed he would gain, and this by his own methods. Christ appears clearly as Redeemer, as Messiah, and people will follow Him in faith.

On Community

A friend told Valeriu: "I have the impression, Valeriu, that you focus on the spiritual problems, on the inner personal life, and you neglect the social aspect of Christianity." Valeriu answered:

The solution that Christians give to humanity is Christian spirituality, and this is an integral conception on life. It is not allowed to limit ourselves to an inner life, neglecting our brethren, but we cannot tailor a world without having a spiritual life. Christian spirituality means the government of the Holy Spirit. Our inner spiritual labors are a preparation for spiritual living in society. Jumping over them means going toward disaster, because we leave Christ behind. If Christianity were not inner life also, it would not respect man and it would not know his freedom. Inner life is inherent in social order. Now, however, we are in a moment of great danger. Let us get ready for death, so that we can gain life.

Q. What is the difference between a Christian community and the other societies?

A. A Christian community is based on the Holy Spirit and on love. It is free. It ensures the perfection of man, and also fellowship among people. A Christian community is not collectivist fiction, nor individualist tyranny, but truth and love, freedom and work.

Q. What is the idea of Christian property?

A. It is communal.

Q. Is a Christian an owner?

A. He is an administrator.

Q. Is it good to live out of mercy?

A. Mercy will never perish, but it is not good for society to be divided into givers and receivers of mercy, because those who receive mercy could be humiliated in their dignity of humans. Mercy is an individual act. Reciprocal help is specific for a community. Fairness and justice belong to politics. However, even in the most perfect humanity, mercy will continue to be one characteristic for relationships among people.

Q. What's your opinion about man's exploitation of man?

A. Man's exploitation of man is terrible; this presupposes a materialist and egoistical individualist-bourgeois society, and it has no tangency with Christianity. However, man can be exploited even more terribly by the state; this presupposes a tyrannical, determinist, materialist, and anti-Christian society."

Q. It turns out that productivity and creation are superior in individualistic societies precisely by their materialistic instincts and their egoism. What do you say about this?

A. The capitalists took into account the social sense of the profits only when they were constrained by circumstances; otherwise, they would have exploited workers mercilessly. Individualism can be a corrective, an alternative to collectivism, just as collectivism can be a corrective and an alternative to individualism. The game of freedom must be moral, and the game of the authority must also be moral. Only the free, conscientious community which is dominated by holy values, can reconcile the conflict between individualism and collectivism.

Q. Is a community about interests or about generosity?

A. It is about consciences, knowledge, and lucidity; this is because it is the only formula which gives spiritual satisfaction and also solves material aspects of life. Through community, life and society are developed in solidarity and harmoniously.

Q. Does an individual have freedom, initiative, and dynamism in a community?

A. On the one hand, an individual gives everything to the community; on the other hand, the community offers him complete freedom of work and creation. A community can only be alive and fruitful through the enthusiasm of all persons who compose it.

Q. Who decides in a community?"

A. I believe that decisions must be catholic.[3] A community is in the service of the people, and the people must decide. The leaders and the elites must have the people's adherence.

Q. Should the universal community be centralized?

A. Communities must develop naturally. However, there is also need for a conscience of a universal community and for a way to participate in it, but not by control and centralized planning, because we would thus get to tyranny.

Q. Who are the spiritual enemies of a Christian community?

A. Evil, sin, passion, egoism, greed, avarice, vanity,

---

3   The term "catholic" here has the meaning found in the Creed: "I believe in a holy, catholic, and apostolic Church..." The Greek origin of the word is the combination of the two terms, *kata* (according to) and *holos* (whole). The Greek phrase *katholou* emphasizes the togetherness of the church as a body that has only one head, Christ.

envy, the tendency to dominate, laziness, indifference, ignorance, angst, disobedience, incorrect-
ness, unbelief.

Q. Who are the material enemies of a Christian community?

A. Matter is not the enemy, but the erroneous understanding and use of matter; the vital necessity
is not the enemy, but the de-naturation of necessities. Laws and forms are not evil, but their *ab-
solutization*; ideas are not evil, for they are good,
but in their place and time; life is not an enemy,
because life is the purpose of our existence, but
the egoist and badly understood life.

Q. Who are the external enemies of a Christian
community?

A. There are individual interests which oppose the
community because of egoism or vanity, interests
that are organized collectively to defend egoism and vanity, and, finally, vanities and egoism
which are organized politically and undermine a
Christian community.

Q. What should Christians do being faced with so
many enemies?

A. They should fight, dare, and face all who oppose
good and truth, responding to individuals,
organizations, and all anti-Christian political
structures.

Q. Should they then reach political power?

A. They should impose respect and freedom from

political power! A people with a living Christian conscience will also have a government on Christian principles. The community should not be confused with the state, though, so that we would avoid arriving at tyranny and abuses.

Q. What is there to do?"

A. We must form people's Christian conscience.

Q. But there are too many Christians who do not understand the meaning and the sense of a Christian community!

A. Unfortunately, this is true. Today's baptized children do not have the spiritual training of the catechumens or of the penitents of the past.

Q. Has the new wine of the Gospel ever had new barrels that could match its quality?

A. There have been people who experienced holiness, there have been societies that labored for justice, but there remains much to do. Christianity cannot declare itself satisfied with any number of saints, or any number of monasteries, but rather with a Christian way of life and a Christian society.

Q. Do you give trust to people?

A. Yes, but also responsibility.

Q. Don't we encounter the risk to fall into historicity?

A. Man cannot be saved without God. History cannot be accomplished without transcendent aspiration; this is why faith is the basis of the entire Christian world. We need grace, we thank God that he has given us grace, and, at our turn, we attempt to fulfill our role as people. We have been saved through Christ; it remains to be saved by our acts."

On Marxism

Q. Valeriu, what is Marxism?

A. It is a false Christianity, the counterfeit of Christianity, the materialization of the spirit, the anthropomorphization of God, the rollover of all values, the imprisonment of the world, philosophically and politically. Marxism is a prison. In a Marxist spirit, all values, all reasons, all things, and all actions become prisons for people. Marx refused any transcendence.

Q. What about socialism?

A. Socialism is a strange mixture of communism and materialist bourgeoisie.

Q. And national-socialism?

A. A confused and vague riposte to Marxism.

Q. Is a Christian socialism possible?

A. Christianity is a spirituality before being anything else, but it also has its historical expression. It is in the service of man, so we could speak of a Christian socialism, but we would prefer calling it *communitarianism*, in order to separate it from the Marxist-atheist socialism. The essences of these two concepts are opposed, just as the historical forms which derive from them are contrary, and also their results.

Q. What do you think about the social Christianity of the West?

A. It does not have chances to succeed because it is not strong enough. The world needs living water which could raise it from the dead water of materialism. The world awaits the definition and the creation of an entirely Christian socialism.

Q. Can Marxism be confused with communism or with *sovietism*?

A. Atheism, *scientiphism*, the lawfulness of historical dialectics, class hatred, and the dictatorship of the proletariat are all Marxist principles, and they are at the basis of communism and *sovietism*. There is nothing taking place in the international communist movement outside of Marx."

Q. What novelty did Stalin bring?

A. Stalin is the faithful embodiment of Marxism-Leninism. Mao, Trotsky, Ana Pauker, Gheorghiu Dej, and all those like them are like Stalin. It is a great error to confuse communism with one person; except Marx and Lenin, all communists are the same. The fight should not be with people, but with the communist conception—that's where the poison is!

Q. Is a conflict between communists possible?

A. If Christian love could not eradicate hatred from among people, how will the communist world be, which believes in hatred? The conflicts amongst communists are inherent (and fulminant), but they do not solve problems, but worsen them. Only people's return to Christ can save humanity.

Q. Is the Soviet revolution Russian?

A. The Russians and all soviet peoples are the material with which the architects of communism built the Soviet Empire. Of course, the material has its meaning and importance in a construction, but the concept that was at the basis of the construction is essential. The Russians are the first victims of Marxism. Lenin himself is no longer Russian, but an "illuminist" or a "communard," because his thinking is westernized.

Q. How do you explain Marx's hatred against faith?"

A. Marx denies Christ, but he also denies Moses and any founder of a religion. Marx denies the priority of the spirit over matter. He justifies hatred against religion by the historical ineffectiveness of faith in solving the social problems of the oppressed and exploited people. Thus, he declares that faith is an opium for people, he replaces love with hatred and freedom with the tyranny and the dictatorship of the proletariat. He rejects spirituality, and he thus makes out of nothingness an absolute in the world. Marx becomes the god of the world—he, poor Marx, who was actually amputated spiritually, having a narrow and opaque conception of life, having venom in everything he was doing; a poisoned, possessed, fanatical, limited and unrealistic man.

Q. If Marxism is so obtuse, how do you explain his explosion in the world, which amazes this century and tends to dominate?

A. Marx used major ideas, which can polarize people, but these ideas have a degraded meaning in Marxist context. He speculated all the weaknesses of the bourgeois world, which constituted a cruel reality, and he mobilized the world for revolution. He misled many by the complexity of the notion of historical dialectical materialism. If you do not consider Marx and Marxism or communism in spirit, you run the risk of being tempted by Marxism.

Q. What is most repulsive in communism?

A. Poverty is difficult, man's imprisonment within the system is serious, but there is nothing more terrifying than the determination of conscience, which transforms man into a guided tool.

Q. But has communism no fissures?

A. There are many ideological fissures, but they cannot be evidenced because the communist power does not accept any liberty or any right to criticize or deny communism. The communist tyranny is formidable. An institutionalized system was created which is holding on to power and wants to extend it at any cost. The perspectives of a triumphant communist empire during this century are opening with a darkness that human imagination cannot still suspect. The "reeducation"[4] in Piteşti is a symbol of the communist world.

Q. What future do you see for humanity?

A. God works in the world. Through many sufferings, humanity will be saved and communism will be defeated, but the world has graver problems to solve. The way of life and the orientation must be changed. Communism will disappear, but it is important with what it will be replaced."

On the Present

Q. Valeriu, you often speak of the *present* of Christianity. How do you see it?

4   The experiment of Piteşti was in essence an attempt to commit a crime that had no body: a crime against the soul. I cite here the tremendous book of Dumitru Bacu, *The Anti-Humans: Student Reeducation in Romanian Prisons* (Englewood: Soldiers of the Cross, 1971). He says, "The biological destruction of an adversary no longer satisfies, or pleases; or maybe it does not pay any more. The wrecking of the victim's mind and soul is more appealing and more useful: the destruction of human characteristics; the reduction of man to a level of total animality; a definitive dehumanization that transforms what was human into a docile, malleable protoplasm, instinctively responsive to all the trainer's whims – a zombie" (3). This process was supposed to take place in four steps and used both physical and psychological torture. The "success" was determined by the transformation of the tortured one into a torturer, a "reeducated."

A. Christ is always and everywhere present in history, mystically, secretly, and by the conscience and work of the faithful.

Q. What are the means to make faith actual?

A. There are spiritual means, as, for example, inner life, spiritual endeavors, morality, virtue, battle with sin, inner renewal, spiritual atmosphere, to which are added learning, the word, creation, study, science, arts, work, and others. There are also organizing means, which derive from the first.

Q. Are there still saints in our world?

A. This century has given a cloud of saints and martyrs, but we do not know them. Christ is present and active in today's world through saints, martyrs, confessors, and heroes. But today's Christian world is not solidly joined with its saints because it cannot follow their examples. If contemporary saints lived at the beginning of Christianity, the entire Christian breath would have lived with them, by them, toward them. We are not Christian, this is why we do not know our saints.

Q. What do you understand by saint and holiness?

A. Any man can be a saint. We have saints who pray in the wilderness, saints who witness in the Roman arenas, saints in catacombs and dungeons, saints emperors and heroes, athletes for Christ, saints of mercifulness, clerical and lay saints, and saints from among the people and among the elites. All people in all areas of life are called to holiness, so to a life lived in the light of the Holy Spirit. And a note: those who were sanctified are not necessarily saints, but only invested with the economy of divine grace. The world needs both saints and those who were made saints.

Q. Do you believe that there are hidden hypocrisies in Christianity?

A. Unfortunately, Christians have often explained their own weaknesses and cowardice by all kinds of philosophies and principles. It is not acceptable to say, "I pray, you can die of hunger," or, "I contemplate God, the world can stay in misery." Faith without works is dead.

Q. How should we then understand the words, "Give to Caesar what is Caesar's and to God what is God's"?

A. As long as "Caesar" is pagan and non-Christian, Christianity lives with him peacefully, respecting its field, but keeping the authenticity of faith untouched. For example, in the Roman Empire, there was no compromise regarding faith before the oppressing Caesar, even if this led to crucifixions and arenas with wild beasts. Those who make compromises with the political leaders in history, hiding under the mentioned teaching of the Lord, leave God and also people behind. The identity of Christianity must be maintained and affirmed with wisdom.

Q. Will the world be able to understand and receive authentic Christianity?

A. With difficulty, but it will be able, because this is God's work in communion with people."

On the Crisis

Q. Valeriu, what is the basis of today's crisis?

A. Atheism.

Q. What do you see in today's world?

A. I see an internal chaos, a decomposition that goes toward nihilism, because people are obsessed by the nothingness of matter, the fiction of forms, sensual exhaustion, historicism without transcendence, ceremony without God, consumerism without spirituality, and the falsity hidden under the self-deification of man. Disaster unfolds on all important aspects of human life. Much suffering is necessary for the spiritual reorientation of the world and for the change of its way of being.

Q. Why did God allow the world to enter in the crisis in which it is, after almost two thousand years of Christianity?

A. The crisis is not God's, nor of faith, but rather of the freedom of people's conscience. The people of the last centuries have de-sacralized the world, desolated souls, exacerbated sensuality, and allowed themselves to be prey to the vanity of materialism and atheism. At the same time, satanic forces are sharper and better organized in the 20th century and in the first Christian age. The way in which saints die, killed by the beast,[5] in the 20th century is more draconic, more perverse, more complete, more studied, and more terrible than how the martyrs of the first Christian centuries of the catacombs were murdered. The millions of Christians today are not at the spiritual level of the catacombs, but holiness and martyrdom are greater than any other time during this century by intensity and forms of manifestation.

The enemies of Christianity, those who provoked martyrdom, want to cover its existence now and make Christ forgotten in the world, but they are mistaken and prove to be helpless. They succeeded in having dominion over the world, but they produced saints and martyrs. They succeeded in closing people's mouths, but they could not cover the light of the saints. God works in the world through unfaithful people as well. This is how one may decipher the meaning of the crisis of the 20th century: the cleaning that is necessary for a higher step of spirituality and life.

Q. What are the ways of coming out of this crisis?

A. The return to Christ. It is necessary to have a Christian elite that would not leave the people, but would fight with boldness against all forms of

5   The "beast" refers to the devil as embodied by communism.

oppressing and enslaving it. The people cannot be protected by prayers and alms only, so by empty formalism, but by fight, audacity, and power. This world is under Christ's dominion, and Christians are not allowed to leave it. There is no graver accusation than saying that the Church has left the people, because then it left Christ, regardless of how many dogmas the Church may have established and obeyed.

Q. Why is faith necessary in the world?

A. Because of the wisdom with which God created the world. The world is imperfect, so imperfect that nothing is perfect in it: neither its political, social, and economical institutions, nor its culture, arts, sciences, philosophies, and beliefs. Free and conscientious people, regardless of how much power they may have in the world, can obtain perfection by communion with God only. If you take away this connection with the divine, man falls into bestiality and nothingness. Faith is thus a necessity.

Q. Christianity is discredited by materialists as retrograde, dark, medieval, inquisitorial, Jesuit, and mystifying. What can we answer?

A. The materialism which denigrates Christianity today has science as theoretical basis; well, science is precisely anti-materialistic and discloses that materialism is tyrannical, limited, narcissistic, nihilistic, baleful, and disastrous. The light of materialism is darkness; the orientations of progressivism are against nature; the sensualism of materialism decomposed nature; the humanism of materialism "beastified" the world; the laws of materialism are fictitious, even if they imprisoned humans' thinking for a while. Science reached the limits of material knowledge, and it now anchors the world in the transcendent.

Q. How can one come out of the materialist crisis?

A. Through Christ, but he is not received by today's world; today, no one is willing to change his vision and way of life, even if we go toward disaster. The events are ongoing and can no longer be stopped, even by Christians. However, we have the duty to shout to people, "Stop your debauchery, give up tyranny, make order within yourselves, put limits to your greed, return to nature, give up your vanities, destroy atomic weapons; if you are rationalist, give up rationalism; if you are realist, see spiritual reality; if you have knowledge, anchor yourself in the transcendent! Give yourself holiness from above; this is the only way to be saved. Repent! Call God to make order in yourselves and in your world, on your land and in your sky!" All these things should not be only abstract and moralizing exhortations. Christians are called to be watchful. The world needs Christ, faith, and authentic Christianity.

On the Role of Christianity

Q. Valeriu, what are today's Christian aspirations?

A. Now and in the future, two Christian process-es are necessary: one of re-Christianization of Christians, and another of Christianization of non-Christians. By re-Christianization I under-stand the strengthening of Christian faith, the ef-fort for authentic Christian life, steps for spiritual growth into perfection, into an active and broth-erly Christian community, and into the defini-tion of the formulas of Christian life. However, Christianity has lost its messianic role and no lon-ger has the necessary historic force for polarizing and for deifying the world. In this way, it leaves an empty space for pagans, atheists, and Jews. Who-ever believes without being a missionary has not yet known the beauty of faith.

Q. Do you think that traditionalism, so Christianity as well, means living in the past?

A. Not at all. Christianity is the present, Christ in the present. If life is unique and always new, how could we live in the past? If life reached the cur-rent forms, how could it deny the past? Through tradition, we do not live in the past, but we give continuity to the Holy Spirit, now and unto the ages of ages. With discernment, care, and wisdom, we must learn from tradition what is necessary for the present and for the future.

Q. Do you believe, Valeriu, that we can live in

eschatological perspective, separated from the world, history, and the present times?

A. Such a theory is as absurd as it is hypocritical. Eternity begins now. Only if we live in eternity now can we have it eschatologically; otherwise, we lose it. Thus, Christians make history, but they are not history, because only by aspiring for eternity will they have the light and power to make out of history always new steps, always higher toward God's Kingdom.

Q. What is necessary for building a Christian world?

A. It is good to follow the classic example of the apostolic community: to know well the Christian teaching so that we can see its applicability in the present times; to unite in a work of solidarity, under the light and guidance of the Holy Spirit; to live in a community of love, which would be according to God's will; to pray, to liturgize, to unite with Christ, so that we would be in his Kingdom through his grace and gift.

Q. Valeriu, what are the factors that save the world?

A. We could say that there is only one, God, and we would not be mistaken, because everything comes from him and the world will be perfected through him. However, proceeding thus, we would not understand man, life, and nature in this way. There are then two factors that decide the destiny of the world: God and man, the descent of Christ, and man's aspiration for the sky—the divine grace and man's will. God's cooperation with man is the key for the world's salvation.

Q. Can we present before the world a concrete Christian plan for life and government?

A. Christians propose a spirituality for the world, and the world must find its corresponding forms of life in the present. The establishment of the world on faith is an unceasing refreshing of the Gospel. The apostolic and martyric spirit must remain alive always. Holy aspirations must vibrate continuously in the world. We aspire for a Christian world, burning in the flame of faith and love, following the passions[6] and the martyrdom, glorifying the Resurrection, the Transfiguration, and the Ascension."

---

6 The Passion experienced by Jesus during the Holy Week.

A Guide for Confession[1]

He that is without sin among you, let him first cast a stone at her.

—John 8:7

Verily, verily, I say unto you, that ye shall weep and lament, but the world shall rejoice: and ye shall be sorrowful, but your sorrow shall be turned into joy.

—John 16:20

[1] The following guide for confession was translated from Monk Moise's *Sfântul Închisorilor*. Monk Moise does not mention his source. Most likely, it was compiled by friends of Valeriu Gafencu, who survived detention.

Jesus riseth from supper, and laid aside his garments; and took a towel, and girded himself. After that he poureth water into a basin, and began to wash the disciples' feet, and to wipe *them* with the towel wherewith he was girded.

—John 13:4–5

Now there was leaning on Jesus' bosom one of his disciples, whom Jesus loved.

—John 13:23

A new commandment I give unto you, that ye love one another; as I have loved you, that ye also love one another.

—John 13:34

By this shall all *men* know that ye are My disciples, if ye have love one to another.

—John 13:35

What is Sin?

SIN is the transgression of God's law, willingly or unwillingly, knowingly or unknowingly, in deed, word, or thought.

Sin is dishonoring God: shame, contempt, defamation, repudiation, and injury against the divine being, born out of an egotistical feeling.

Sin is unfaithfulness and mistrust in God, in his law, and too much faith and trust in oneself, to the point where man is a law unto himself. After you have violated God's law, you follow another law, either yours, or the devil's.

Sin is a second crucifixion brought upon the Savior, because all the mockeries and beatings that he received are renewed in sin. The Savior experiences the nails again, the spear, and the thorns because of sin. Now, he is no longer nailed by those who defamed him and shouted, "Crucify him, Crucify him." Now, the nails are administered by those who claim to believe in him, to follow his commandments, to love him. Those who are baptized spit on him now, those who call themselves Christians place on his head the crown of thorns, those for whom he suffered mockeries and beatings, for whom he gave his blood on Golgotha to make them sons of God, to open heaven for them, to crush death and destroy hell, they hit him on the face, nail him, and pierce him with the spear.

Sin is departure from God and approaching the devil, departure from the home of the Father and working in foreign country for the pigs of the devil.

We are the slaves of the one whom we serve,[2] so sin means enslavement to the devil.

When you sin, you no longer consider what God did for you, you are no longer his son, and you no longer think about his justice, which will punish those who sin against his will.

2   Jn 8:34.

In sin, all of God's things work against the purpose for which they were created. The mouth was not made by God to curse our neighbor, but to say things that are helpful for the soul. God did not give you the mind to find arguments that detach you from God, but to find the arguments that bring you closer.

Eyes were not made to behold what brings damage to the soul, but to see God's creations and give him thanks. Similarly ears, hands, and feet were not created to get further from God.

Don't you want to consider God's goodness and long-suffering? You should know that your entire time was given to you so that you gain heaven, and you lose yourself when you think that he will not judge, that he will forgive us anyway, and that others are more evil than you.

The Consequences of Sin

The evil that sin produces:

Through sin, we lose the gift surpassing nature that we have from God. Without this gift, the soul remains misshapen.

Through sin, the Holy Spirit is taken from us and we are no longer recognized as sons.

Through sin, we lose the eternal happiness of heaven; we lose the possibility of union with God and feasting together with the saints; we lose eternal life and rest.

We gain hell, with the unquenchable fire and eternal darkness.

Through sin, we lose all good things we have previously done because God will judge you in what He finds you doing at present.[3]

Through sin, we lose God's help (that is, while you are in sin).

Confession

Aren't you crying, thinking that you have lost heaven?

Aren't you shuddering because of the sorrow you brought to God?

Aren't you dreading hell?

Aren't you looking to regain the state that you lost?

Is it still possible?

Yes! You only need to desire it...

God knew our weakness from the beginning, and he gave us the possibility to cleanse our sins. He knew that man will sin his entire life and that nobody is without mistakes; this is why he told his

3   Justin Martyr attributes this phrase to Christ in his dialogue with Trypho: "In whatsoever things I shall take you, in these I shall judge you." Justin Martyr, *Dialogue with Trypho*. Translated by George Reith. We can find a similar phrase in Clement, in Alexander Roberts, James Donaldson, and A. Cleveland Coxe (eds), *Ante-Nicene Fathers*, Vol. 2 (Buffalo, NY: Christian Literature Publishing Co., 1885.) Revised and edited for New Advent by Kevin Knight. In Clement, the phrase sounds this way, "For by the state in which I find you will I judge."

disciples, "Verily I say unto you, whatsoever ye shall bind on earth shall be bound in heaven: and whatsoever ye shall loose on earth shall be loosed in heaven."[4] This is how the sacrament of confession was instituted.

Confession or repentance is a bath from which the soul comes out relieved of the weight it carried and cleansed from the dirtiness of sins, a bath in which all our filthiness and mistakes are washed and lost.

Confession is a medicine that cures the soul that has been harmed by the devils, a medicine that breaks the poison of sin.

Confession returns sinner from the devil to God and places him back in connection with his Maker.

Confession means bringing the soul to the works and things that are for and according to its nature.

Confession renders a man clean to God.

Confession prepares the soul and the body for receiving the Holy Body and Blood of our Savior, Jesus Christ.

Go to confession four times a year[5] to the same spiritual father.

When you make an examination of conscience, find yourself guilty and don't justify yourself; consider the following points:

---

4   Mt 18:18.
5   The four confessions per year are connected with the four fasting seasons.

- The reason or the purpose with which or for which you sinned. Attempt to avoid that moment the following day.
- The intention you had when you sinned.
- Avoid the circumstances the following day.
- The place where you sinned.
- The degree to which you spread your sin— that is, whether you encouraged others to do it.
- How many times…?

Confession must be made with a broken heart and with regret. Brokenness of heart is the sorrow and pain that you experience when you remember your sin.

This pain does not only consist in resenting sin, sighing, and crying because of it, but also and especially in hating sin.

Regret is the pain experienced by one who repents because he has deprived himself of God's gift and thus received a laborious existence.

The Church has established [the custom of] fasting for seven days before confession, or even less. Those who are sick are exempt.

Write your sins on a piece of paper and read them before your spiritual father. Promise before God that you will no longer do these things.

The Ten Commandments

THE FIRST COMMANDMENT:

I am the Lord your God, do not have other gods
before me.

—Exodus 20:2–3

- Do you believe in God?
- Do you believe in the Holy Trinity?
- Do you worship God?
- Do you love Him?
- Do you know Him? Have you labored to find out something about God from the Holy Scriptures, religious books, or some other place?
- Do you believe in magic?
- Did you go to fortunetellers or soothsayers?
- Do you practice spiritism?
- Do you believe in dreams? Believe in God only.
- Do you honor a being or a thing more than God?
- Do you value money, food or wine, a woman or a man, more than God?
- Have you ever grumbled against God?
- Have you despaired because of a problem, grief, or any other evil that came upon you?
- Have you opposed Christian truths and teachings?

- Have you read books against faith?
- Have you given such a book to someone else to read?
- Have you been at the meetings of unbelievers?
- Have you read their books and magazines with the purpose to find another truth than the one of the Church?
- Have you defended unbelief or the sects of Mohammedism?
- Have you given gifts to sectarians?
- Do you follow any vain or pagan beliefs, such as: "My day will be bad because I met a priest," or "I met a chimney sweep, so I'll have a good day," or looking whether people crossed your path with an empty or full bucket?[6]

Is God the center of your preoccupations?

- Have you always placed your hope in God?
- Do you believe that heaven and hell are real?
- Do you believe that there will be a judgment?
- Do you trust God's goodness too much, and so you are not afraid of judgment?
- Do you believe that God can no longer forgive you because of the multitude and gravity of your sins?
- Have you always asked for God's help?

6 The popular belief is that your day will be good if someone with a full bucket crosses your way, but it will be bad if the bucket is empty.

- Did you pray regularly, in the evening, in the morning, and at lunchtime?
- Do you go regularly to church?
- Are your thoughts focused on God only in prayer and in church?
- Do you remember God during the day?
- Do you give thanks to God after each of your works?
- Have you asked for God's help before doing something?
- Do you ever say prayers just out of habit or because you want to be done with it?
- Do you think of other things during prayer?
- Do you ever have thoughts that you would no longer be able to be saved?
- Did you postpone your salvation for old age?
- Do you attempt to be late for church?
- Do you listen to the service attentively?
- Do you laugh, talk, or look around for people in church?

THE SECOND COMMANDMENT:

Thou shalt not make unto thee any graven image, or any likeness of any thing that is in heaven above, or that is in the earth beneath, or that is in the water under the earth: thou shalt not bow down thyself to them, nor serve them.

—Exodus 20:4–6

- Do you consider that some people are great and that they have the same importance as the Savior, people such as [great] philosophers or the leaders of [other] religions?
- Do you believe in the holy icons?
- What kind of veneration do you have for them?
- Do you ever believe that the icon is truly the saint that it depicts?
- Do you put your faith in people (your wife, your husband, your child, etc.)?
- Do you worship an object, money, food, drink, or other pleasures?
- Is your mind your only law: you do only what it tells you?

THE THIRD COMMANDMENT:
Do not take the name of the Lord thy God in vain.
—Exodus 20:7

- Have you ever cursed about God the Father or the Savior Jesus Christ?
- Have you cursed about angels or archangels?
- Have you cursed about the holy Virgin?
- Have you cursed about saints, the Church, Easter, candles, icons, the Cross, and other such things?

- Have you taken a false oath using the name of the Lord?

- Have you sworn on your eyes, your life, or the salvation of your soul? For the Savior said: your word should be yes and no; for anything beyond this comes from the devil one.[7]

- Have you told people to go to the devil or have you said it to yourself?

- Do you have the custom to curse those who do evil to you? The Savior taught us to pray for them.

- Have you made a false oath?

- What about true oaths?

- When making oaths, do you use the expression *zău*, which is the abbreviation of "on my God"?[8]

THE FOURTH COMMANDMENT:
Remember the Day of the Lord, work six days, and celebrate on the seventh.

—Ex 20.8–11

The Day of the Lord is on Sunday. All of the feasts instituted by the Holy Church over the course of the year have the same importance as Sunday.

---

7   Mt 5:37.
8   In Romanian, the word for "God" is *Dumnezeu*. When people promise that they are telling the truth, they sometimes use the expression *zău*, meaning "I swear."

- Have you observed all Sundays and all feasts?
- Have you gone to church on all of these days?
- Have the people from your home gone to church? Have you kept them at home for some reason?
- Have you given work to others during these days? Do you go to church too late?
- Do you celebrate the Day of the Lord properly? Or is it just a usual day for you, or a day for parties? Do you go to church in the morning? Do you read useful books after lunch, books that edify your soul?
- Do you take care of your soul during this day more than during other days?
- Have you organized or participated in communal work on Sundays?[9]
- Do you act unbecomingly in church?
- Have you blasphemed the Church and the servants of the holy altar?
- Do you honor priests as God's servants? Do you scoff them? Do you gossip, speaking of their sins?
- Do you pray for them? Do you listen to them?

---

9   The Romanian word is *clacă*, which designates collective work done by peasants to help one another, which is often followed by a small gathering filled with songs, jokes, and stories. The expression "*lucru de clacă*" is used to point to work done without desire and also badly.

THE FIFTH COMMANDMENT:

Honor your father and your mother, so you are well and your years are many.

—Exodus 20:12

- Have you beaten your parents or your parents-in-law?
- Have you cursed them or persecuted them?
- Have you listen to their advices?
- Have you cheated them in some matter?
- Have you taken advantage of their trust?
- Did you help them when they were in need?
- Have you had memorial services[10] after their death?
- Have you helped your brothers and sisters?
- Have you taken care of your wife and children? St. Paul says, "But if any provide not for his own, and specially for those of his own house, he hath denied the faith, and is worse than an infidel."[11]
- Have you beaten your wife? Have you behaved badly with her? Have you cursed her?
- Did you honor your husband? Did you love your wife or your husband as yourself?

---

10 Memorial services are offered in memory of the deceased after their death. In the belief that all people are living in Christ, the Orthodox Christians continue to pray for their departed ones.

11 1 Tim 5:8.

- Have you cheated on your husband or your wife?
- Have you made their lives more difficult? Do you nag?
- Do you pay sufficient attention to the spiritual needs of those in your home?
- How have you behaved with your spiritual parents—godparents, professors, priests? Have you respected them and have you helped them?
- Were you insolent and stubborn with your parents?
- Have you upset them? Angered them?
- Have you said bad things about them or have you scoffed them?
- Have you laughed at their helplessness?
- Have you taken care so that they could do their religious duties?
- Were you ashamed of them?
- Have you spent your money on useless things (tobacco or other pleasures) and thus you made your family miss useful things?

If you are a parent:

- Have you guided your children on the path of the Church, with your deeds and your words?
- Have you given them bad example, with fights, drunkenness, foul language, lies, theft, dishonesty, slandering, or laziness?

- Do you live in concubinage and the children see this?
- Have you punished them for bad acts: quarrels, lies, fighting, or theft? Have you spared them out of pity [from a punishment they deserved and would have benefited them]?
- Have you prayed for your children, wife, husband, brothers, sisters, and parents?
- Were you too harsh or too gentle with your children?
- Did you have bad servants, who could teach your children bad things for the soul?

If you are a tutor:

- Have you fulfilled all your material and moral obligations to the child?

If you are a master (employer):

- How did you behave with your servants or your apprentices?
- Have you paid their income honestly? Have you cut parts of it for some reason?
- Have you encouraged them to do their religious duties?
- Have you encouraged them to commit any sin?

If you are a servant (employee):

+ Have you listened to your masters, employers, etc.?
+ Have you accomplished all of your duties in earnest?
+ Have you worked without diligence?
+ Have you stolen from them?
+ Have you talked about their domestic affairs?

THE SIXTH COMMANDMENT:
Thou shall not kill.

—Exodus 20:13

+ Have you ever killed, willingly or unwillingly?
+ Do you have thoughts about murder or about revenge? Have you praised someone who killed?
+ Do you desire someone's death, to take that person's wealth, wife, husband, etc.?
+ Have you beaten anyone?
+ Have you threatened anyone?
+ Do you hate anyone; are you in peace with all your acquaintances?
+ Do you wish death, injury, or evil on someone?
+ Do you rejoice when evil things happen to your brethren?
+ How do you behave with those around you?

- If you are a man, did you agree to the abortion of your child?
- If you are a woman, have you willingly had a baby aborted?
- Have you attempted to commit suicide, directly or indirectly?
- Have you hunted?[12]

THE SEVENTH COMMANDMENT:
Thou shalt not commit adultery

—Exodus 20:14

The one who is not married commits fornication; the one who is married, adultery.

- Have you committed fornication or adultery?
- Do you live with a concubine?
- Do you sin against nature by masturbation or homosexuality?
- Do you desire to fornicate with someone else's husband or wife?
- Do you look for occasions for fornication?
- Do you think about shameful things too often?

---

12   Note from the editor: While, to my knowledge, hunting is not considered a sin, the fact that Gafencu lists it here is interesting. First, we can say that he may consider the sport of hunting as problematic, because it involves the killing of a being for pleasure. Second, listing hunting as a sin further shows the kindness of his heart.

- Do you look for occasions to recall such scenes?
- Do you want to see shameful parts of the body?
- Do you speak about shameful things?
- Have you read books that gave you sexual pleasure?
- Have you encouraged someone else to commit this sin?
- Have you caused someone to sin by the way you dressed or adorned yourself?

THE EIGHT COMMANDMENT:
Thou shalt not steal

—Exodus 20:15

The priest cannot forgive the theft without restitution; return what you have stolen and then confess.

- Have you stolen money or other objects from the state, society, or any man?
- Have you injured others?
- Have you compensated the injured one?
- Have you taken care of someone's wealth after it was entrusted to you?
- Have you returned money or other objects that you have borrowed?
- Have you accepted stolen things?
- Have you returned what you found?

- Have you dishonestly adjusted the borders of your land with your neighbor?
- Have you encouraged someone else to do this?
- Have you charged interest that is too high?
- Have you falsified merchandise; have you sold it as good merchandise?
- Have you cheated on the scale or with money?
- Have you taken things from your lessers by force?
- Have you taken bribes?
- Have you taught your children to steal?
- Do you have thoughts of becoming rich by dishonest means?

THE NINTH COMMANDMENT:
Thou shalt not bear false witness against thy neighbor

—Exodus 20:16

- Have you perjured?
- Have you lied?
- Have you given false testimony?
- Have you been honest with your brother?
- Have you lied to him?
- Have you carried lies?
- Have you spread rumors from person to person?

THE TENTH COMMANDMENT:
Thou shalt not covet anything that your brother has.

—Exodus 20:17

- Have you desired the wife, the daughter, the husband or the son of your brethren?
- Have you desired your neighbor's wealth?
- Have you desired the social status of the one above you?
- Have you hated a neighbor because of this?
- Have you desired the house, the land, the vine, or the good of your brother?

The Seven Deadly Sins

PRIDE

- Pride is the source of all wickedness of the soul; it is a spiritual greed because of which the devils fell from God's gift.
- Are you proud or conceited?
- Do you believe too much in your beauty or wealth; have you boasted about them?
- How do you behave with those above you?
- Do you despise anybody?
- Do you talk to anyone?
- Are you false, hypocritical (you say one thing and do another)?
- Have you praised yourself by works, words, or clothes?

- Have you said something in order to be praised?
- Have you slandered your brethren to diminish his honor and valor and praise only yourself?
- Have you endured the insult of the one who insulted you?
- Have you forgiven those who were upset with you?
- Have you shown off your knowledge?

GREED

- From abstract, egoism is materialized by greed.
- St. Apostle Paul has this perspective when he says that greed is the root of all evil.
- Are you greedy for food or drink?
- Do you want to gather wealth or other things?
- Are you greedy when you save money? Have you cheated your neighbor because of this?
- Have you eaten or drunk in secret?
- Did you eat during feasts before the Holy Liturgy?
- Have you eaten carrions?

LAZINESS

- Laziness is the non-use of the bodily and

spiritual powers that God gave us to use in our lives.

- ✦ Are you lazy?
- ✦ Do you lose your time without working?
- ✦ Do you get busy with evil or vain things (the adornment of the body etc.)?
- ✦ Do you pray regularly?
- ✦ Do you take care of your soul?
- ✦ Do you do your duty as a clerk, worker, or servant?
- ✦ Do you force the people beneath you to do your job?
- ✦ Have you searched for a more forgiving confessor?
- ✦ Have you done your canon after confession?

ANGER

- ✦ Anger is established on the pivot of greed as well.
- ✦ When man cannot accomplish his cravings, he is angry because he is prevented from his evil purpose.
- ✦ Man may have anger only against sin.
- ✦ Did you do evil in anger, such as swearing, fights, etc.?
- ✦ Are you angry often? For how long? Do you know that St. Paul said, "Let not the sun go down upon your wrath"?[13]

13   Eph 4.26.

- Are you upset with anyone?
- Have you hit anyone, with a bat or with a slap?
- Have you upset or scolded someone without reason, maliciously?
- Have you desired evil for the one who wronged you? What about the one who benefited you?
- Were you angry with your neighbor because he was better than you? Have you envied him? Do you regret it?
- Have you shed anyone's blood (in drunkenness)?
- Have you fought in a duel?
- Have you prayed (in anger) that your enemies would receive evil?

AVARICE

- Avarice could be material and spiritual.
- It is material when man does not want to take care of the poor one bodily, and it is spiritual when he does not want to guide the ignorant out of evilness.
- Are you stingy?
- Have you not helped a neighbor with necessary things out of avarice?
- Have you helped the poor one?
- Have you invited poor or rich to your table? Do you know that the Savior encourages us

to invite to our table those who cannot invite us back?

- Do you sell too high?
- Do you cheat?
- Do you regret when you do something good?
- Do you eat only a little or dress poorly (yourself and your family) in order to get rich?
- Do you avoid caring for the health of your children, wife, parents, brothers, in order to avoid spending money?

ENVY (*leading to quarrels or malice*)

It takes place when the one who is furious cannot overcome his obstacles with his anger, and, not being able to do something else, sweetens his heart in the passions of envy, so that he would cover the spiritual and material honesty and worthiness of his neighbor and rise himself up.

- Are you in conflict with anyone?
- Do you like quarreling?
- Do you hate anyone?
- Do you scoff?
- Do you give sly advice?
- Do you envy anyone now?
- Do you speak with everyone?
- Have you nicknamed anyone?
- Have you stirred up the pot among brothers?
- Do you envy someone because he is better

than you or he is more honored, wealthier, better placed socially, etc.?

FORNICATION

This is also greed, but not of a spiritual or material nature, but of a sentimental kind. The sin of fornication, like no other sin, is done in the body. The body is the temple of the Holy Spirit. (You can commit fornication by looking at or hearing things which would make you sin—even by eating, sleeping too much, speaking, etc.).

- Have you fallen into fornication?
- What about adultery?
- Do you enjoy watching or reading books that make you sin in your thoughts? Do you enjoy listening to or saying shameful words, dirty talk? Know that Saint Paul says that neither filthiness, nor foolish talking, nor jesting, which are not convenient, should be heard from your mouths.[14]
- Do you like to engage in idle talk? Or do you just enjoy talking?
- Are you overpowered by any passion?
- Do you eat or sleep too much? You know that the same apostle Paul said, "All things are lawful unto me, but all things are not expedient"?[15]

14   Eph 5:4.
15   1 Cor 6:12.

+ In your house, do you have paintings with naked people [depicted therein]? Do you look at them with passion?
+ Have you fornicated with blood or spiritual relatives (godchildren, godparents)?
+ Have you touched someone else's body because you were overcome by the passion of fornication?
+ Have you desired to see shameful parts of the body?

Outrageous sins

VOLUNTARY MURDER

+ Have you killed anyone?
+ Did you attempt to kill?
+ Do you want to kill anyone?
+ Do you want to get revenge by taking someone's life?
+ Have you beaten anyone?
+ Have you harangued or threatened anyone?

SODOMY (*intercourse against nature*)

+ Man with man or with any kind of animal?
+ Man with woman against nature?
+ Masturbation: have you masturbated?

INJUSTICE OF EMPLOYERS

- Have you beaten children, old people, or orphans?
- Have you withheld pensions or salaries, regardless of reasons, either as compensation for a broken thing or for any other reason?
- Have you withheld portions of money unjustly?
- Have you always paid for the work done by others?

OPPRESSION OF WIDOWS, ORPHANS, DISABLED PEOPLE, OR THE POWERLESS

- Have you beaten children, old people, or orphans?
- Have you mocked them?
- Have you persecuted the one less than you?
- Have you laughed at crippled or disabled people?
- Have you harassed them?
- Have you had the duty to help them and you did not do it?
- Have you helped those who were not under your responsibility, or did you pass by them, like the priest or the Levite in the gospel of the Good Samaritan?[16]
- Have you made the blind fall by guiding him badly?

---

16   Lk 10:25–37.

- Have you mocked the helpless, the deaf, the stuttering, the lame, the crippled, or the blind?

Duties for the spiritual life of your neighbor
- Keep another from sinning: have you done it or not?
- Teach the ignorant.
- Give good advice to the one who needs it.
- Pray to God for others.
- Succor the grieving.
- Suffer with patience when you are wronged.
- Forgive the errors of others.

Commandments concerning the bodily life of your neighbor
- Feed the hungry: did you do it or not?
- Quench the thirst of the thirsty.
- Clothe the naked.
- Care for the sick.
- Take in and feed strangers.
- Visit those in prison.
- Bury the dead.

Actions that lead others to sin
- When you advise someone to sin.
- When you command to someone to sin.
- When you agree with another to sin.
- When you help someone to sin.

- When you praise someone who sins.
- When you can, but you do not want to stop someone from sinning.
- When you know it, but you don't tell someone his sin (you should tell him).

Sins against the holy spirit

- Dismissing God's grace and having too much trust in yourself.
- Believing that God does not have the power to forgive you—this is a very great sin.
- Believing that you are everything and that God has no power in the world.
- Not trusting God.
- Being against the Truth established by the Holy Church (not believing in a dogma).
- Giving up the Orthodox Church. Avoid these sins because the Savior says, "But he that shall blaspheme against the Holy Spirit hath never forgiveness, but is in danger of eternal damnation."[17]

The nine commandments of the church

- Go to the holy church on all Sundays and established feasts.
- Observe the four Lenten periods each year.
- Respect the clergy.

17   Mk 3:29.

- Confess your sins during the four Lenten periods.
- Avoid the heretics.
- Pray for the leaders of the country and of the Church.
- Do not have a wedding or parties in Lent.
- Protect the Church from having its goods taken away.
- Observe Lent and the [periods of] prayer that the local bishop decrees during difficult times.

Various sins
- Not fulfilling your promises.
- Did you fulfill the promises taken before God, yourself, and your neighbor?
- Did you do the penitential rule received at [your last] confession?
- Stealing sacraments: did you lie during confession? Did you avoid saying something for whatever reason?

Advice
- Go to confession at least four times per year, during the Lenten periods.
- Fast before confession.
- Keep the same spiritual father.
- Examine your conscience before going to confession.

- Write your sins on a piece of paper, so you would not forget them. Then burn it immediately.
- Confess not only what you have done, but also the sins of your heart.
- Do not hide any sin.
- Make peace with the one who wronged you.
- Avoid the occasion to sin.
- Leave sin behind—promise that you will no longer sin.
- Regret the sins you did.
- Avoid them as much as possible.
- Have communion only if you feel pure. Otherwise, you will be condemned.
- Faithfully observe the rule given you by your confessor.
- Accuse yourself for every sin you did.

ﻉ

Each one of us has a purpose, but we have to remain under the advice of our spiritual father, who removes our unwise will, making space for God's will in each of us. The spiritual father reveals God's intentions in us. If we do not stay under his advice, we can fall into errors greater than passions.

I sense as a friend every soul that sends me a single thought of love. I desire and I pray that each friend copies this guide for confession. I wrote it as I could, in all rush, from my pure desire to send you this guide for confession.

With all my love,
Valeriu